LAW, CRIME AND LAW ENFORCEMENT

TRANSNATIONAL GANGS: THE MS-13 GANG AND OTHERS

Law, Crime and Law Enforcement

Additional books in this series can be found on Nova's website under the Series tab.

Additional E-books in this series can be found on Nova's website under the E-books tab.

Social Issues, Justice and Status

Additional books in this series can be found on Nova's website under the Series tab.

Additional E-books in this series can be found on Nova's website under the E-books tab.

LAW, CRIME AND LAW ENFORCEMENT

TRANSNATIOANAL GANGS: THE MS-13 GANG AND OTHERS

MICHELE L. MONTEITH
EDITOR

Nova Science Publishers, Inc.
New York

For permission to use material from this book please contact us:
Telephone 631-231-7269; Fax 631-231-8175
Web Site: http://www.novapublishers.com

Library of Congress Cataloging-in-Publication Data
Transnational gangs : the MS-13 gang and others / editor, Michele L.
Monteith.
p. cm.
Includes index.
ISBN 978-1-61728-917-0 (hardcover)
1. Gangs--United States. 2. Gangs--Central America. 3. Gangs--Latin
America. 4. MS-13 (Gang) I. Monteith, Michele L.
HV6439.U5T727 2010
364.106'6--dc22
2010026192

Published by Nova Science Publishers, Inc. ✣ New York

CONTENTS

PREFACE

Street gangs have long been a concern to policy makers. The more recent emergence, growth, and expansion of two Latino street gangs, the Mara Salvatrucha (MS-13), and the 18th Street Gang, have raised concern among policy makers for several reasons. Reports suggest that these gangs are engaged in criminal enterprises normally associated with better organized and more sophisticated crime syndicates and perhaps most disturbingly for policy makers in a post 9/11 world, alarms have been sounded in some circles that international terrorist organizations like al-Qaeda could exploit alien and narcotics smuggling networks controlled by these gangs to infiltrate the U.S. This book provides an overview of the MS-13 and M-18 gangs, examines how these gangs are different from other gangs and organized crime groups, discusses what constitutes a transnational gang and the various federal responses to these gangs.

Chapter 1- Two predominantly Latino gangs, Mara Salvatrucha (MS- 13) and the 18th Street gang (M-18), have raised concern among policy makers for a number of reasons, including (1) membership in these gangs has spread from the Los Angeles area to other communities across the United States; (2) these gangs are considered "transnational," primarily because MS-13 and M-18 cliques are being established in Central America and Mexico; (3) there are reports suggesting that these gangs are engaged in criminal enterprises normally associated with better organized and more sophisticated crime syndicates; and (4) MS-13 and M-18 gang members may be involved in smuggling operations and, by extension, could potentially use their skills and criminal networks to smuggle terrorists into the United States. To date, however, no evidence exists establishing a link between MS-13 and M-18 members and terrorists.

Nevertheless, some observers maintain that these two gangs may develop the capacity to become organized criminal enterprises capable of coordinating illegal activities across national borders. Yet, others find them to be no more criminally organized or sophisticated than other street gangs. At issue for Congress is whether the MS-13 and M-18 gangs constitute an emerging transnational criminal threat.

The federal response to the MS-13 and M-18 gang problem has largely involved the enforcement of criminal and immigration laws, including the deportation of alien gang members. More recently, federal efforts have focused on prosecuting gang members under the

Racketeer Influence and Corrupt Organizations (RICO) statute. Deported alien gang members have established MS-13 and M-18 gang cliques in their home countries, and some experts suggest that U.S. deportation policies have effectively transported U.S.-styled gang culture to parts of Central America and Mexico. Moreover, evidence shows that deported alien MS-13 and M-18 gang members have established a "revolving door" migratory pattern of repeat illegal reentry into the United States, raising concerns that these "migratory" alien gang members may become involved in narco-trafficking, smuggling, and other criminal activities along the U.S.-Mexico border.

Chapter 2- During its second session, the 111th Congress is likely to maintain an interest in the effects of crime and gang violence in Central America, and on the expanding activities of transnational gangs with ties to that region operating in the United States. The violent Mara Salvatrucha (MS-13) and its main rival, the "18th Street" gang (also known as M-18) continue to threaten citizen security and challenge government authority in Central America. Gang-related violence has been particularly acute in Honduras, El Salvador, and Guatemala, which have among the highest homicide rates in the world. Governments in those countries appear to have moved away, at least on a rhetorical level, from repressive anti-gang strategies. However, they have yet to implement effective anti-gang policies that include an emphasis on prevention and rehabilitation of former gang members.

U.S. officials have expressed concerns about the expanding presence of the MS-13 and M-18 in cities across the United States, as well as reports that these gangs may be evolving into more sophisticated transnational criminal enterprises. Between February 2005 and September 2009, U.S. officials arrested some 2,572 alleged MS-13 members in cities across the United States, many of whom were subsequently deported. Evidence suggests, however, that previously deported members of both the MS-13 and the M-18 often reenter the United States illegally across the U.S.-Mexico border.

Several U.S. agencies have been actively engaged on both the law enforcement and preventive side of dealing with Central American gangs. An inter-agency committee worked together to develop a U.S. Strategy to Combat Criminal Gangs from Central America and Mexico, first announced at a July 2007 U.S.-Central American Integration System (SICA) summit on security issues. The strategy, which is now being implemented, states that the U.S. government will pursue coordinated anti-gang activities through five broad areas: diplomacy, repatriation, law enforcement, capacity enhancement, and prevention.

Chapter 3- Thousands of gang members in the United States belong to gangs such as MS-13 and 18th Street that are also active in Central American countries. Federal entities with responsibilities for addressing Central American gangs include the National Security Council (NSC); the Departments of Homeland Security (DHS), Justice (DOJ), and State; and the U.S. Agency for International Development (USAID). GAO was asked to review federal efforts to combat transnational gangs. This book addresses (1) the extent to which the federal government has developed a strategy to combat these gangs, and (2) how federal agencies have implemented the strategy and other programs to combat these gangs, coordinated their actions, and assessed their results. GAO examined federal agencies' antigang plans, resources, and measures; interviewed federal, state, and local officials in seven localities representing varying population sizes and geographic regions; and interviewed U.S. and foreign officials in El Salvador and Guatemala where U.S. agencies have implemented antigang programs. The results of these interviews are not generalizable.

Chapter 4- Another kind of war within the context of a "clash of civilizations" is being waged in various parts of the Americas, Africa, Asia, Europe, the Middle East, and elsewhere around the world. Some of the main protagonists are those who have come to be designated as first-, second-, and third-generation street gangs, as well as their various possible allies such as traditional Transnational Criminal Organizations (TCOs). In this new type of war, national security and sovereignty of affected countries is being impinged every day, and gangs' illicit commercial motives are, in fact, becoming an ominous political agenda.

Rather than trying to depose a government with a major stroke (*golpe* or coup) or in a prolonged revolutionary war, as some insurgents have done, gangs and their allies (the gang phenomenon) more subtly take control of territory and people one street or neighborhood at a time (*coup d' street*) or one individual, business, or government office at a time. Thus, whether a gang is specifically a criminal or insurgent type organization is irrelevant. Its putative objective is to neutralize, control, or depose governments to ensure self-determined (nondemocratic) ends. This objective defines insurgency, a serious political agenda, and a clash regarding the authoritative allocation of values in a society.

The purposes of this monograph are to (1) introduce the gang phenomenon as a major nonstate player and a serious threat in the global and regional security arenas;(2) examine the gang phenomenon in Central America in general and in El Salvador, Mexico, Jamaica, and Brazil more specifically; and (3) summarize the key points and lessons and make brief recommendations. These cases demonstrate the analytical commonalities of various types of gang activities as they contribute to the instabilities that lead to the erosion of national security, nation-state sovereignty, the processes of state failure, and the struggle between democratic and criminal values.

In: Transnational Gangs: The MS-13 Gang and Others
Editor: Michele L. Monteith
ISBN: 978-1-61728-917-0

Chapter 1

THE MS-13 AND 18TH STREET GANGS: EMERGING TRANSNATIONAL GANG THREATS?*

Celinda Franco

SUMMARY

Two predominantly Latino gangs, Mara Salvatrucha (MS- 13) and the 18th Street gang (M-18), have raised concern among policy makers for a number of reasons, including (1) membership in these gangs has spread from the Los Angeles area to other communities across the United States; (2) these gangs are considered "transnational," primarily because MS-13 and M-18 cliques are being established in Central America and Mexico; (3) there are reports suggesting that these gangs are engaged in criminal enterprises normally associated with better organized and more sophisticated crime syndicates; and (4) MS-13 and M-18 gang members may be involved in smuggling operations and, by extension, could potentially use their skills and criminal networks to smuggle terrorists into the United States. To date, however, no evidence exists establishing a link between MS-13 and M-18 members and terrorists.

Nevertheless, some observers maintain that these two gangs may develop the capacity to become organized criminal enterprises capable of coordinating illegal activities across national borders. Yet, others find them to be no more criminally organized or sophisticated than other street gangs. At issue for Congress is whether the MS-13 and M-18 gangs constitute an emerging transnational criminal threat.

The federal response to the MS-13 and M-18 gang problem has largely involved the enforcement of criminal and immigration laws, including the deportation of alien gang members. More recently, federal efforts have focused on prosecuting gang members under the Racketeer Influence and Corrupt Organizations (RICO) statute. Deported alien gang members have established MS-13 and M-18 gang cliques in their home countries, and some experts suggest that U.S. deportation policies have effectively transported U.S.-styled gang culture to

---

* This is an edited, reformatted and augmented edition of a United States Congressional Research Service publication, Report RL34233, dated January 22, 2010.

parts of Central America and Mexico. Moreover, evidence shows that deported alien MS-13 and M-18 gang members have established a "revolving door" migratory pattern of repeat illegal reentry into the United States, raising concerns that these "migratory" alien gang members may become involved in narco-trafficking, smuggling, and other criminal activities along the U.S.-Mexico border.

INTRODUCTION

Street gangs have long been a concern to policy makers. The more recent emergence, growth, and expansion of two Latino street gangs, the Mara Salvatrucha (MS- 13)[1] and the 18th Street Gang (also known as the Mara 18 or M-18), have raised concern among policy makers for several reasons.[2] First, membership in these gangs has spread from the Los Angeles area to other communities across the United States. Second, there are concerns that these gangs are becoming increasingly transnational, primarily because MS-13 and M-18 cliques are being established in Central America[3] and Mexico. Third, there are reports suggesting that these gangs are increasingly engaged in criminal enterprises normally associated with better organized and more sophisticated crime syndicates. Fourth, and perhaps most disturbingly for policy makers in a post- 9/11 world, alarms have been sounded in some circles that international terrorist organizations like al-Qaeda could exploit alien and narcotics smuggling networks controlled by these gangs to infiltrate the United States. To date, however, no evidence suggests that these gangs and international terrorist groups are cooperating with one another.[4] Nonetheless, at issue for Congress is whether the MS-13 and M-18 gangs constitute an emerging transnational criminal threat.

This chapter provides an overview of the MS-13 and M-18 gangs,[5] examines how MS-13 and M18 gangs are different from other gangs and organized crime groups, and discusses what constitutes a transnational gang. The report also explores whether MS-13 and M-18 gangs are transnational gangs, and discusses the various federal responses to these gangs. The report concludes with a discussion of selected issues that may be of interest to Congress.

DEFINING THE ISSUE

There is no single definition of what characteristics constitute a transnational gang.[6] Various characteristics have been used to distinguish and identify transnational gangs, including (1) gangs that are criminally active and operational in more than one country; (2) gangs that are involved in criminal activities committed by gang members in one country that may be planned, directed, and controlled by gang leaders in another country; (3) gangs that tend to be mobile and adapt to new areas; and (4) the criminal activities of such gangs tend to be sophisticated and transcend national borders. For a gang to be considered transnational, the gang would likely exhibit more than one of the aforementioned characteristics; however, with respect to the MS-13 and M-18 gangs, much of the literature characterizes these gangs as transnational because they are present and criminally active in more than one country.

BACKGROUND ON THE MS-13 AND M-18 GANGS

Two predominantly Latino gangs, MS-13 and M-18, have taken a place on the national policy agenda, as membership in these gangs has spread from Los Angeles to other parts of the United States. Although street gangs are largely an urban phenomenon, MS-13 and M-18 cliques have emerged among disaffected Latino youth in suburban and rural areas across the country. According to a national gang survey, the MS-13 and M-18 gangs have an established presence in Washington DC; Northern Virginia; certain cities in Maryland; Nashville, Tennessee; New York, New York; Houston, Texas; and other rural and urban areas.[7] The M-18 gang is a much larger gang than the MS-13 in terms of overall membership, with approximately 30,000 to 50,000 members nationwide, compared with 8,000-10,000 MS-13 members nationwide in 2009;[8] however, the MS-13 gang has generated greater media coverage and congressional attention.[9]

Federal law enforcement authorities have targeted MS-13 and M-18 alien gang members for deportation, an action that some argue has contributed to the development and proliferation of U.S.-styled gangs in Central America and Mexico.[10] Although membership in the MS-13 gang is largely Salvadoran and membership in the M-18 gang is largely Mexican, both gangs have recruited members in the United States from other Central American countries. Some have argued that as a result of this inter-mixed membership, both gangs have established gang cliques in El Salvador, Honduras, Guatemala, and Mexico that are modeled on, and perhaps linked to, U.S. MS-13 and M-18 gangs.[11] According to some, Central American and Mexican MS-13 and M-18 gangs maintain elements often referred to as "LA-style" gang culture commonly found among Los Angeles-based gangs.[12] Because the gangs are present in multiple countries, some contend that these gangs are transnational.

Origins of Mara Salvatrucha (MS-13)

The MS-13 gang reportedly originated in Los Angeles in the 1980s. During this period, thousands of Salvadorans fled the civil war in their country.[13] By the end of the 1980s, some estimates indicate that more than 300,000 Salvadorans had settled in Los Angeles.[14] One hypothesis on the gang formation asserts that Salvadorian immigrants during this period banned together and formed the MS-13 gang. [15]

MS-13's early membership is reported to have included former guerrillas and Salvadoran government soldiers whose combat experience during the Salvadoran civil war contributed to the gang's notoriety as one of the more brutal and violent Los Angeles street gangs.[16] Moreover, the gang developed a widely reported reputation of employing unusual methods of violence, including using machetes in gang attacks.[17] Despite the gang's reputation, sources in law enforcement indicate that little evidence exists to substantiate that the MS-13 gang is more violent than other street gangs.[18]

Origins of 18th Street Gang (M-18)

The 18th Street gang (M-18) was originally formed by Mexican migrants in the 1960s in the Rampart neighborhood of Los Angeles who were blocked from joining other native-born Mexican-American gangs.[19] The 18th Street gang grew by expanding its membership to other nationalities and races, and it was among the first multiracial, multiethnic gangs in Los Angeles.[20]

Are MS-13 and M-18 Different from Other U.S. Street Gangs?

According to research, gangs can be characterized as either first-generation, second-generation, or third generation.[21] First-generation gangs are characterized as traditional street gangs. These gangs are turf-oriented and localized, lack sophistication, engage in unsophisticated criminal activities, and tend to have a loose leadership structure. First-generation gangs participate in "opportunistic criminal activity and intergang rivalry."[22]

Second-generation gangs are characterized as having an organized structure similar to a business. They tend to "assume a market rather than a turf orientation."[23] Second-generation gang activities tend to be drug-centered. Moreover, these gangs tend to operate in broader areas and have a centralized leadership.[24]

Third-generation gangs are characterized as highly sophisticated, "mercenary-type group[s] with goals of power or financial acquisition and a set of fully evolved political aims."[25] Third- generation gangs tend to operate in a global environment and "may embrace quasi-terrorism or true terrorism" to advance their goals.[26]

Most urban gangs fit into the first- and second-generation characterizations.[27] Some researchers believe, however, that the MS-13 and 18th Street gangs *in some Central American countries* have some of the characteristics of a third-generation gang.[28] Although such researchers do not link the MS-13 and 18th Street gangs to terrorist groups, they assert that these gangs and terrorist groups have some similar characteristics, such as having "a propensity for indiscriminate violence, intimidation [and] coercion [that] transcend[s] borders, and target[s] nation-states."[29]

In the United States, the MS-13 gang does not appear to have escalated to a third-generation gang; however, evidence suggests that the gang's presence in multiple states, as discussed above, and its criminal activities indicate that the gang is evolving. This point is underscored by the 2004 National Drug Intelligence Center (NDIC) threat assessment report. Despite the generally loose organization of the MS-13 gang, the NDIC 's 2004 report warned that the gang was increasing its coordination between chapters in Los Angeles, Washington DC, Northern Virginia, and New York, perhaps indicating efforts to create a national command structure.[30]

STREET GANGS, TRANSNATIONAL GANGS, AND ORGANIZED CRIMINAL ENTERPRISES

As previously mentioned, no single, widely accepted definition of what constitutes a transnational gang exists, and the lines between street gangs, transnational gangs, and organized criminal enterprises can be blurred. The following section highlights some of the major distinctions between these criminal groups.

How Are Transnational Gangs Different from Street Gangs?

Generally, most researchers agree that the *primary* distinction between transnational gangs and other domestic street gangs is that transnational gangs are criminally active and operational in more than one country. In some cases, they may be characterized as gangs in which members in one country typically commit crimes that could have been substantially planned, directed, and controlled by the gang's leaders in another country.[31] Other researchers characterize transnational gangs as "very mobile, highly adaptable to new geographic areas, and [maintaining] connections in their native countries."[32]

As previously mentioned, most street gangs are either first- or second-generation gangs. Transnational gangs, however, share some of the same characteristics as a third-generation gang. For example, transnational and third-generation gangs tend to operate in a global environment— that is, their criminal activities transcend borders. Moreover, with respect to their criminal activities, both types of gangs tend to have a level of sophistication that closely resembles organized criminal syndicates.

What Is an Organized Criminal Enterprise?

Organized crime is defined by the Federal Bureau of Investigation (FBI) as any group having a formalized structure whose primary objective is to obtain money through illegal activities.[33] Such groups tend to have a vertical hierarchy, strong leadership, sanctions for failure of its members to abide by codes of loyalty, and a level of entrepreneurial expertise. The specific criminal acts that organized criminal enterprises tend to engage in are specified in statute as part of the Racketeer Influenced and Corrupt Organizations (RICO)[34] and the Violent Crimes in Aid of Racketeering (VICAR)[35] statutes. According to the FBI, organized criminal enterprises maintain control of their illegal activities through tactics such as actual or threatened violence, graft, and extortion. The activities of organized crime syndicates can be sophisticated enterprises capable of adversely effecting localities, regions, and, in some cases, the nation as a whole.

How Are Street Gangs Different from Organized Crime?

With the exception of third-generation gangs, street gangs are generally considered distinct from organized criminal enterprises because they typically lack the hierarchical leadership structure, organizational structure, capital, and manpower required to run a sophisticated criminal enterprise. Street gangs are generally more horizontally organized, with lots of small cliques with their own leadership and no centralized, overarching leadership setting strategy and enforcing discipline. Most often, gang leaders are easily and quickly replaced by other gang members without disruption to the gang's activities.

Street gangs often engage in some of the same types of criminal activity as organized criminal enterprises, but generally at much lower levels and not always strictly driven by entrepreneurial objectives. Research indicates that most street gang crime tends to be opportunistic and improvised. As previously discussed, street gangs tend to be concerned with issues such as neighborhood territory or turf protection and maintaining respect for the gang and its members.

Another key difference between street gangs and organized criminal enterprises is evident when comparing federal prosecutions of organized crime with federal prosecutions of street gang offenses. In gang cases, the prosecution can face obstacles prosecuting these cases under the existing RICO statute, which has been instrumental in hampering, if not dismantling, organized criminal enterprises. Generally, when a federal criminal gang case is being developed for a RICO prosecution, prosecutors must demonstrate that the crimes were committed or were connected to the interests of a criminal enterprise.[36] Although many cases against organized criminal enterprises have been successfully prosecuted under the RICO statute, it is more difficult to develop a RICO case against street gangs.

MS-13 Gangs and Organized Crime

The Washington Office on Latin America (WOLA)[37] researched and interviewed MS-13 members in the Washington DC area over a period of a year.[38] As a result of the research, WOLA issued a report in February 2007, in which it concluded that MS-13 and M-18 members in the Washington DC area were not engaged in a systematic effort to become more involved in organized crime. The report found that the area's MS-13 membership was sizable, although the members' criminal activity was largely limited to petty theft and neighborhood extortion. The analysis of the MS-13 gang in the Washington DC area concluded that active gang "hot spots" existed, but that the *maras* did not constitute a major public security issue.

In contrast to the WOLA report, law enforcement officials point to evidence that the Washington DC area's gangs are indeed criminally active and may show signs of increasing criminal sophistication.[39] For example, they assert that in the Washington DC area, Immigration and Customs Enforcement (ICE) agents reported arresting 233 known violent gang members, 190 of which were MS-13 members, in 2006. In addition, a milestone case for the federal prosecution of gang members under the RICO statute was based on MS-13 members committing crimes in the Washington DC area. Two MS-13 gang members were convicted of murdering six people and attempting to kill four others in a federal case prosecuted in Prince George's County, Maryland.[40] The two convicted MS-13 members were part of an indictment brought against 22 MS-13 members. Successfully prosecuting a racketeering conviction against MS-13 members is seen by some analysts as evidence that the gang's criminal activities are becoming increasingly organized and sophisticated.

ARE MS-13 AND M-18 TRANSNATIONAL GANGS?

As previously mentioned, MS-13 and M-18 gangs are generally considered to meet at least one of the characteristics attributed to transnational gangs—they are present in more than one country. And with respect to the MS-13 gang, evidence suggests that the gang is becoming more organized, which is another characteristic of transnational gangs. For example, recent criminal cases involving MS-13 defendants have included information and testimony that gang members in Maryland were in telephone contact with other MS-13 members in cities across the country and, on occasion, with MS-13 members in El Salvador.[41] Criminal cases brought against MS-13 also indicate that the gang members share information and, in some cases, that cliques in one area have loaned weapons to members of an MS-13 clique in another area.[42] This evidence of contact, communication, and perhaps criminal cooperation is seen by some experts as an indication that the MS-13 gang could evolve from a street gang into a more sophisticated transnational gang.[43]

Some critics contend that the transnationalization of the MS-13 and M-18 gangs began with the deportation of alien gang members from the United States in the mid-1990s. They assert that the increase in deportations of aliens to Central America and Mexico initiated by changes made to immigration law in the mid-1990s[44] led to the establishment of MS-13 and M-18 cliques in those countries. However, the actual number of alien gang members that were deported is not clear from the immigration removal data. Others assert that these countries already had a gang problem and that MS-13 and M-18 cliques were not formed in Mexico and Central American countries as the result of a gang migration or as an effort to establish new gang franchises or otherwise further gang-related criminal enterprises of the U.S.-based gangs.[45] Instead, deported gang members banded together for social and economic advantage, as a way to compete with existing Central American and Mexican gangs, and to survive in a foreign environment on income obtained through familiar criminal means. Once established, these MS-13 and M-18 cliques recruited new local members, and their ranks continued to be supplemented with new native recruits and additional U.S. alien gang deportees.[46]

Prevalence of MS-13 and M-18 Gangs in Central America

Estimates of the number of MS-13 and M-18 gang members in Central America and Mexico range from 70,000 to 100,000, depending on the source of the information, and at least one report claims that MS-13 and M-18 cliques have established a growing presence in 24 of Mexico's 32 states.[47] MS-13 and M-18 gangs in Central America and Mexico are reported to have larger total memberships and are reportedly more structured than their U.S. counterparts, although these differences are difficult to corroborate.[48]

Evidence of a Transnational Gang Threat?

Since the 9/11 terrorist attacks, attention has been focused on securing the U.S. borders and ports of entry. The long, porous southern border with Mexico is considered a vulnerability, in part because of the relative ease with which illegal aliens, narcotics, and contraband are smuggled into the United States, as well as the extent to which people cross into the United States illegally. Policy makers have been concerned about human and narcotic smuggling rings and the possibility that such profit-driven enterprises could be used by terrorists to enter the country undetected.[49] Although there is no data linking the MS-13 and M-18 gangs with organized smuggling activities, there are concerns that the gangs may become more organized and sophisticated in their criminal activities.

FEDERAL RESPONSE TO GANGS

In general, gang-related crimes fall within the jurisdiction of state and local law enforcement. As gangs have spread across the country, and as their threat has become more national in nature, the interest in finding adequate solutions to the problem has increasingly included all levels of government. In the mid- to late1980s and early 1990s, Congress passed legislation federalizing certain gang-related crimes and providing additional penalties for individuals convicted under these laws.[50] Moreover, in the mid-1990s, Congress passed legislation that changed immigration enforcement laws and made more aliens deportable.[51] In addition, the federal government has taken an active role in helping state and local jurisdictions develop anti-gang responses through support for research on gangs and through grant programs to help jurisdictions develop effective gang prevention and intervention strategies.[52]

Two federal agencies are directly involved in the fight against gangs through the enforcement of criminal and immigration laws. The Department of Justice (DOJ) administers the primary federal efforts to investigate, apprehend, and prosecute domestic criminal gang activities. The Department of Homeland Security (DHS) also plays a role through the enforcement of immigration and criminal law. The following two sections discuss some of these DOJ- and DHSled initiatives. The sections do not discuss gang/crime prevention initiatives.[53]

Department of Justice Agencies and Initiatives

Several federal offices and bureaus within DOJ are engaged in fighting gang criminal activities. For example, as the primary criminal investigative agency in the federal government, the Federal Bureau of Investigation (FBI) is responsible for investigating criminal violations of federal law. The Drug Enforcement Agency (DEA) is the lead agency charged with enforcing the controlled substance laws and regulations of the United States. The agency is also charged with stemming the production, manufacture, distribution and trafficking into the country of illicit drugs and, as such, is the lead agency in several initiatives. In its role as federal prosecutor, the U.S. Attorney's Office (USAO) Criminal Division prosecutes federal gang cases investigated by the FBI and the Bureau of Alcohol, Tobacco, Firearms and Explosives (ATF). In addition, the USAO Criminal Division has a section known as the "gang squad," which is a part of ATF-headed gang task force. Because gang crime often involves the use of guns, the ATF is directly involved in investigating both domestic and transnational gangs. These and other DOJ agencies also participate in anti- gang task forces established to combat gang crime and various forms of international organized crime, some of which specifically target transnational gangs.

FBI's MS-13 National Gang Task Force

The FBI established the MS-13 National Gang Task Force (NGTF) in December 2004 to coordinate the investigative efforts of federal, state, and local law enforcement agencies targeting MS-13 gang members and their associates. By increasing and speeding the flow of intelligence and information to support and coordinate investigative efforts, the MS-13 NGTF provides information to help law enforcement agencies identify trends in gang activities.[54]

According to DOJ, the MS-13 NGTF is designed to manage the flow of information nationally and internationally to help coordinate investigations. Reportedly, the FBI's MS-13 NGTF works with international law enforcement agencies to collect and share intelligence on transnational gangs.[55] The FBI has also launched the Central American Fingerprint Exploitation (CAFE) initiative, which is designed to merge criminal records from Central American partner law enforcement agencies with FBI fingerprint database to help identify gang members with criminal histories.[56] According to the FBI, more than 100,000 fingerprint cards (sets of fingerprints) have been entered into the database, and of those, 20,000 cases have come to the attention of law enforcement agencies in the United States.[57]

FBI's Safe Streets and Violent Crimes Initiative

The Safe Streets and Violent Crimes Initiative (SSVCI) permits the Special Agent in Charge of each FBI field division to establish long-term, proactive task forces focused on reducing violent crime. [58] The task forces place specific emphasis on the identification of major violent street gangs and drug enterprises of national scope by applying the same methods used to successfully fight traditional organized crime. According to FBI testimony before the Senate Judiciary Committee, one of the first gangs to be targeted by the gang task force was the MS-13 gang.[59] Moreover, the work of the task force enabled the U.S. Attorney for the Central District of California to successfully use statutes to prosecute the leaders of the 18th Street Gang and the Mexican Mafia.[60]

According to the FBI, the task force concept increases the effectiveness and productivity of limited personnel and logistical resources, avoids duplication of investigations, and expands cooperation and communication among law enforcement agencies. In response to the threat from gangs, the FBI established the Safe Streets Violent Gang Task Forces (SSVGTF) to coordinate the efforts of law enforcement at all levels of government and to use the same statutes, intelligence, and investigative techniques against violent gangs that are used to fight organized crime. The FBI's Safe Streets and Gang Unit administers 160 task forces nationwide.[61]

FBI's National Gang Strategy

The FBI's National Gang Strategy (NGS) incorporates the investigative and prosecutorial practices that have been successful in the Organized Crime/Drug Program National Strategy.[62] The NGS promotes the sharing of information among federal, state, and local law enforcement agencies, which in turn helps the FBI identify violent gangs with coordinated investigations that support prosecutions. The NGS is a component of DOJ's overall Anti-

Violence Crime Initiative, which is designed to promote cooperative strategies and information sharing on gang-involved offenders among corrections, parole and probation, and law enforcement agencies.

FBI's National Gang Intelligence Center

In 2005, pursuant to P.L. 108-447, Congress provided funding for the FBI to establish the National Gang Intelligence Center (NGIC), a coordinating center for information and intelligence on gangs that could be shared with law enforcement. According to testimony at a congressional hearing, the NGIC "will enable the FBI and its local, state, and federal partners to centralize and coordinate the national collection of intelligence on gangs in the United States and then analyze, share, and disseminate" the information to the law enforcement community.[63] Staffed with intelligence agents, the NDIC provides law enforcement agencies with information on gang growth, criminal activities, gang migrations, and emerging trends based on national and international gang intelligence.[64]

Bureau of Alcohol, Tobacco, Firearms and Explosives (ATF)

The ATF is the principal law enforcement agency within DOJ responsible for enforcing federal criminal laws and regulations relating to the firearms and explosives industries. Working directly and in partnerships with other law enforcement agencies at all levels of government, the ATF investigates and works to reduce crime involving firearms and explosives, act of arson, and illegal trafficking of alcohol and tobacco products. ATF is the lead DOJ agency in the Regional Area Gang Enforcement (RAGE) Task Force, which includes agents and officers from ATF, FBI, ICE, and other state and local law enforcement agencies. In addition, ATF is the lead agency in the 15 Violent Crime Impact Teams (VCITs), 13 of which focus on gang activity tied to homicides.[65] The ATF is also involved in several federal task forces and leads the investigations of violent gang crime through its firearms tracing system and the National Tracing Center (NTC), as well as through the Regional Crime Gun Centers (RCGCs) located in major cities plagued by gang violence. The ATF also provides national training programs for federal, state, and local law enforcement officers and prosecutors as part of the Project Safe Neighborhoods (PSN)[66] program on street-level gun recoveries, enforcement tactics, and firearms identification and tracing procedures.

Gang Targeting Enforcement Coordinating Center

The national Gang Targeting Enforcement Coordinating Center (Gang TECC) is a unified federal effort to coordinate anti-gang efforts among several DOJ agencies.[67] Gang investigators from the ATF, Federal Bureau of Prisons (BOP), FBI, U.S. Marshals, the DEA, and ICE share intelligence to coordinate anti-gang investigations at the federal, state, and local levels. In addition, investigative efforts are coordinated with prosecutors from the U.S. DOJ Criminal Division to provide direct support, guidance, and assistance with anti-gang efforts.

DOJ Joint Initiative with El Salvador

In February 2007, the Attorney General announced an initiative to collaborate with the government of El Salvador to fight transnational gangs operating in El Salvador, Central America, and Mexico. The initiative, led by the FBI and the Department of State (DOS), provides assistance to El Salvador's civilian police (Policia Nacional Civil, or PNC). As part of the initiative, a transnational Anit-Gang (TAG) unit was created to pursue and prosecute gang members. The TAG units include investigators from the PNC in El Salvador, imbedded prosecutors from El Salvador's Attorney Generals office, special FBI teams assigned to El Salvador, and support from DOS.[68] FBI agents provide training, information sharing, and other support to increase the capacity of PNC detectives to identify, arrest, and prosecute gang offenders. In a second part of the initiative, the FBI will accelerate the implementation of the CAFE initiative (described above), designed to improve the identification, tracking, and apprehension of gang members.

Department of Homeland Security Agencies

Agencies within the Department of Homeland Security (DHS) also engage in federal anti-gang initiatives. Efforts to deport alien gang members who reside illegally in the United States, or who have committed certain crimes, are a significant part of ICE's strategy. Customs and Border Protection (CBP) leads the charge of enforcing immigration and criminal law at the border.

Immigration and Customs Enforcement (ICE)

ICE initiated Operation Community Shield in February 2005 to address the threat posed by the MS-13 gang.[69] This initiative was based on a 2003 ICE assessment of violent street gang activity in the United States. The ICE assessment identified MS-13 as a street gang "having a presence across the United States, a significant foreign-born membership and history of violence. [70]

The initiative was expanded to include other violent gangs. Under the expanded initiative, ICE has investigated the violent criminal activities of several other gangs, including the 18th Street gang. Since the initiative was launched, more than 15,000 gang members and associates have been arrested, representing over 1,000 different gangs, of which more than 6,000 were criminal arrests and 9,000 were administrative immigration arrests.[71] In conjunction with the gang arrests, ICE has seized 876 firearms (as of January 4, 2010).[72]

Customs and Border Protection

According to CBP, the MS-13 gang is engaged in smuggling drugs and illegal aliens, as well as extortion, kidnapping, and murder for hire.[73] The border patrol has been required to collect intelligence information on the MS-13 gang since October 2004.[74] In FY2006, the border patrol apprehended 294 gang members nationally; of those, 208 were MS-13 members.[75] Moreover, in 2006, the border patrol's Rio Grande Valley sector (in Texas) had the highest number of MS-13 apprehensions nationally.[76]

SELECTED ISSUES FOR CONGRESS

Whether the MS-13 and M-18 gangs pose a threat to the domestic security of the United States is not definitively known. Moreover, with the exception of established MS-13 and M-

18 cliques in Central America and Mexico, it is not altogether clear whether these two gangs pose a particular transnational threat. It is noteworthy, however, that despite the transnational aspects of the MS-13 and M-18 gangs—they are criminally active in more than one country—in many respects, they are no different that other domestic street gangs. Nevertheless, MS-13 and 18th Street gang members pose a criminal threat to the communities where they reside and conduct their criminal activities. In addition, evidence suggests that previously deported members of these two gangs reenter the United States illegally across the U.S.-Mexico border.

Criminal Prosecution of Gang Members

Federal efforts to dismantle and deter criminal street gangs include a number of approaches. One approach to gang crime would lower the threshold for the number of individuals required to constitute a "criminal street gang," thus making it easier to apply additional charges to certain felony offenses. Building on existing law, another response to the gang problem would impose harsher prison sentences for gang-related federal felony offenses. This section will consider these and other federal proposals to address the gang problem.

Sentencing Enhancements and Mandatory Minimums

Proposals have been made to permit or require (in the case of mandatory minimum sentences) longer sentences for those convicted of certain serious federal crimes if they are committed by gang members. Proponents of these types of anti-gang measures argue that such enhanced federal penalties are needed to address the rising gang crime in communities across the country. They contend that longer sentences could deter violent gang-related crime and encourage greater cooperation by gang members with law enforcement and prosecutors—the rationale being that gang members facing a longer prison sentence will be more inclined to cooperate with prosecutors, providing useful information on the gang and its members in exchange for a shorter prison sentence.[77]

Critics of harsher criminal penalties and mandatory minimum sentences argue against these proposals on several fronts. On the broadest level, some critics oppose the further federalization of laws that have been traditionally under the sole jurisdiction of states and localities. These critics cite the growing number of new federal laws, recently estimated at almost 4,450.[78] They also argue that state and local law enforcement officers have the necessary experience and local intelligence sources to investigate and prosecute gang crimes, which may vary greatly by state, region, and locality, whereas federal sources are strained as they cope with investigating and prosecuting national threats.[79] Opponents of mandatory minimum sentences for gang-related crime also point to the greater expense of imprisonment versus the costs of prevention and rehabilitation efforts.[80] Moreover, critics question the deterrence effect of these harsher penalties, arguing that in certain situations, individuals break the law *notwithstanding* severe criminal penalties.[81] In addition, researchers have often noted that imprisonment can serve to strengthen gang allegiances and function as criminal "finishing schools" for gang members.[82]

Gang-Specific RICO Act Provisions

Under current law, the RICO statute provides for prosecution in cases where the goal is to effectively dismantle the criminal enterprise. As previously mentioned, federal prosecutors have successfully prosecuted organized criminal syndicates under the RICO statute and have recently sought the prosecution of several MS-13 gang members.

Proponents of expanding the federal RICO statute to include violent gang-related crimes argue that having gang-specific RICO provisions is necessary to pursue violent gangs such as the MS-13 and M-18 gangs. They contend that such provisions would provide law enforcement with an important tool to investigate and prosecute gang-related crime. Moreover, they contend that gang- specific RICO provisions will help federal prosecutors pursue gangs that have moved drug trafficking and other criminal activity onto federal land to avoid detection and state or local prosecution.

Opponents argue that existing RICO laws are sufficiently broad to provide for the successful prosecution of gang-related crime. Despite the obstacles faced in developing successful RICO- gang cases, gang members have recently been successfully convicted under existing federal RICO statutes. The recent conviction of three MS-13 gang members in Hyattsville, Maryland,[83] adds credence to the argument that existing RICO laws are sufficient. In addition, other gang cases have been federally prosecuted under RICO statutes in the past, and several states have enacted state-versions of RICO-like laws for prosecuting gang conspiracy cases.[84]

Immigration Enforcement and Border Security[85]

As previously discussed, one of the more overt tools used to dismantle gangs has been the enforcement of immigration law. Because street gangs such as MS-13 and M-18 may have some number of foreign-born members, immigration enforcement (i.e., deportation) is a direct method for disrupting these gangs. ICE "sweeps" of alien gang members have netted both MS-13 and M18 members with criminal histories, as well as alien gang members without criminal histories.

Some critics contend that the gang problem cannot be resolved through immigration enforcement alone. They argue that not all gang members are foreign nationals, and such a policy could lead to ethnic and racial profiling. Furthermore, they assert that deportation is not a long-term solution to the gang problem because evidence suggests that alien gang members are crossing illegally back into the United States. They also argue that by deporting alien gang members, the United States is deporting its gang culture to other countries.

Data Improvements on Transnational and Alien Gangs

Data on gangs in general, and the MS-13 and M-18 gangs specifically, are limited. The organizational strength of MS-13 and M-18 gangs across national borders, and their ability to carry out serious criminal offenses, is an important indicator of their potential threat to the domestic security of the United States. Currently, the National Youth Gang Center (NYGC)[86] authors a survey on youth gangs. While the survey includes responses from major law enforcement jurisdictions (i.e., urban areas), it does not include every rural and suburban law enforcement jurisdiction. As gangs spread to nontraditional areas in the country (i.e., rural and suburban areas), the need to capture data in these areas becoming increasingly critical. More detailed reporting of gang crime could help develop more refined information on the incidence of such crime and the migration patterns of these gangs.

CONCLUSION

The concept of transnationalism was coined in the aftermath of the First World War in a discussion of America's composition as an immigrant "melting-pot" and the implications for assimilation and maintaining a cultural connection to one's previous homeland.[87] More recently, the concept of transnationalism has been used to describe the ideals of globalization, the free movement of people, the sharing of culture, and improved communications across national boundaries, and generally has been considered a positive concept. However, in the context of crime policy, particularly after the terrorist attacks of September 11, 2001, transnationalism has assumed a more ominous connotation, and the potential for gangs in the United States to become transnational has become a concern to lawmakers.

The phenomena of gangs is complex, multifaceted, and constantly evolving. The allure of gangs has traditionally been thought to be a response to issues associated with poverty and disparities in social opportunities. Although gangs have always been in existence, gangs today are more violent, more organized, and more widespread.

The problems associated with stemming the spread and sophistication of MS-13 and M-18 gang activities may reflect current limitations to addressing what is now generally considered a multinational and regional problem. The problems associated with these two gangs cannot be solved by arrests, prosecution, imprisonment, and immigration enforcement alone. The fact that these two gangs exist and operate outside of the United States and beyond the reach of domestic law enforcement agencies indicates that domestic responses may not fully address the broader problems presented by these gangs, and that a multilateral and multinational approach in combination with domestic efforts may be warranted. Recent efforts of various federal agencies, working together with the governments of other countries, particularly El Salvador, on their problems with MS-13 and M-18 and other gangs, indicate that the federal response is moving toward a bilateral approach to addressing the problem.

Whether the problem of these two gangs continues to be approached as a domestic social issue, a domestic security issue, a multinational/regional issue, or a combination of these concerns has yet to be determined. Congress may consider these and other issues in shaping a legislative response to this complex policy concern.

End Notes

[1] The word *mara* is a Spanish word for a gang, and *marero* means gang member. These terms are more commonly used in El Salvador. In the recent literature on Latino transnational gangs, the term *maras* has come to refer specifically to the MS-13 and M-18 gangs.

[2] Although there are other domestic gangs with transnational members, MS-1 3 and M-1 8 are the focus of this chapter because they have been the most prominently discussed by the media and policy makers.

[3] For more information, see CRS Report RL341 12, *Gangs in Central America*, by Clare Ribando Seelke.

[4] Personal communication with Brian Truchon, FBI, Director of the MS-13 Gang Task Force, June 2007.

[5] This chapter addresses the domestic aspects of the MS-13 and M-18 gangs. The international perspective on these and other gangs in Latin America is beyond the scope of this chapter. For information on the international perspective, see CRS Report RL341 12, *Gangs in Central America*.

[6] Transnational gangs are not a new phenomena in the United States and have included gangs composed of members of Asian, Russian, African, Serbian, Bosnian, Jamaican, and other races, ethnicities, and nationalities. Some of these transnational gangs have evolved into highly organized and sophisticated criminal enterprises known for influencing government officials and the judiciary in the countries in which they operate. In the United States, the most well-known example of this type of crime syndicate is the Mafia, or *La Cosa Nostra*, composed of members of Sicilian descent.

[7] The National Youth Gang Center (NYGC) survey does not include gang-specific estimates. More information on the NYGC analysis is available at http://www.iir.com/NYGC/nygsa, January 21, 2010.

[8] The National Alliance of Gang Investigators Association (NAGIA), *2005 National Gang Threat Assessment*, p. 31, available at http://www.ojp.usdoj.gov/BJA/what/2005_threat_assesment.pdf, January 21, 2010.

[9] Although it is unclear whether the MS-13 gang engages in more violent or different types of criminal acts than M-18 or other gangs, MS-13 cliques are reported to have presence in almost every state. According to Federal Bureau of Investigation (FBI) estimates, the MS-13 gang is active in 42 states and the M-18 gang is active in 20 states. U.S. DOJ, FBI, Headline, *The MS-13 Threat: A National Assessment*, at http://www.fbi.gov/page2/jan08/ms13_011408.html.

[10] Guatemala Human Rights Commission, Fact Sheet: Gangs in Guatemala, at http://www.ghrc-usa.org/Publications/ GangFactSheet.pdf , January 22, 2010; Gloria Goodale, "LA's Latest Export: Gangs," *Christian Science Monitor*, February 10, 2006.

[11] Ibid.

[12] These adopted LA-style gang cultural elements include distinctive modes of dress, such as wearing certain colors or bandanas or certain sports jerseys; using gang-specific identifying hand signs; getting gang-identifying tattoos; using gang-specific graffiti to mark a gang's territory; participating in gang-specific initiation practices, often referred to as getting "jumped-in" or "beaten-in," where initiates are beaten by current gang members for a specified length of time or in a particular way; and being required to commit a violent criminal act in order to prove one's loyalty to the gang. Ibid.

[13] Hundreds of thousands of Central Americans, including Salvadorans and Guatemalans, migrated to the United States during the 1980s, fleeing civil war, repression, and economic devastation that plagued the region. See *Central Americans and Asylum Policy in the Reagan Era*, by Susan Gzesh, Migration Policy Institute, Migration Information Source, April 1, 2006, and CRS Report 98-3, *The Nicaraguan Adjustment and Central American Relief Act: Hardship Relief and Long-Term Illegal Aliens*, by Larry M. Eig (available from the author).

[14] Mary Helen Johnson, "National Policies and the Rise of Transnational Gangs," *Migration Information Source*, Migration Policy Institute, April 1, 2006.

[15] Fred Burton, "Mara Salvatrucha: The New Face of Organized Crime?" Stratfor, March 29, 2006, available at http://www.stratfor.com/mara_salvatrucha_new_face_organized_crime January 22, 2010.

[16] *The Economist*, "Special Report: Criminal Gangs in the Americas," January 7, 2006, p. 23.

[17] Ibid.

[18] Personal communication with Wesley D. McBride, Executive Director of the California Gang Investigator's Association.

[19] Al Valdez, Investigator, Orange County, California, District Attorney's Office, "18th Street: California's Most Violent Export," NAGIA, Gang Profiles, available at http://www.streetgangs.com/topics/2002/18thexport.html, January 22, 2010.

[20] Ibid.

[21] See, for example, John P. Sullivan, "Third Generation Street Gangs: Turf, Cartels and Net Warriors," *Crime and Justice International*, vol. 13, issue 10 (November 1997), hereinafter cited as "Sullivan." This concept is further explored in *Street Gangs: The New Urban Insurgency*, by Max G. Manwaring, pp. 8-11, available at http://www.strategicstudiesinstitute.army.mil/pdffiles/PUB597.pdf, and Robert J. Bunker, ed., "Non-State Threats and Future Wars" (Portland, OR: Frank Cass, 2003), pp. 48-50.

[22] See Sullivan.

[23] Ibid.

[24] Ibid.

[25] Ibid.

[26] See Sullivan.

[27] Ibid.

[28] John P. Sullivan, *Transnational Gangs: The Impact of Third Generation Gangs in Central America*, July 1, 2008. Available at http://www.airpower.maxwell.af.mil/apjinternational/apj-s/2008/2tri08/sullivaneng.htm#Sullivan, January 22, 2010.

[29] Ibid., p. 9.

[30] U.S. DOJ, National Drug Intelligence Center, *National Drug Threat Assessment*, June 2004, p. 10.

[31] James O. Finckenauer, "Meeting the Challenge of Transnational Crime," *National Institute of Justice Journal*, July 2000, p. 3.

[32] Claude Arnold, U.S. ICE, Human Rights violators and Public Safety Office, "Immigration Authorities and Gang Enforcement," *United States Attorneys' Bulletin*, May 2006, p. 42.

[33] U.S. Department of Justice, Federal Bureau of Investigation, Investigative Programs, Organized Crime, Glossary, available at http://www.fbi.gov/hq/cid/orgcrime/glossary.htm, January 22, 2010.

[34] 18 U.S.C. § 1961(1).

[35] 18 U.S.C. § 1959.

[36] To investigate and prosecute organized criminal enterprises, the FBI relies on the Enterprise Theory of Investigation (ETI). Under this investigative model, the investigation and prosecution are focused on the criminal activities of the entire criminal enterprise rather than on just those committed by any single individual. This approach targets all aspects of the criminal operation to disrupt and ultimately destroy the entire structure of the enterprise. In fact, an essential part of the ETI strategy is to show that the individuals in such an organization commit criminal acts "solely to benefit their criminal enterprise." Using the ETI, the FBI can support the prosecution of the criminal enterprise under RICO statutes or its related statute, VICAR, and seize the enterprise's assets to seriously disrupt or dismantle entire criminal organizations.

[37] WOLA is a non-governmental organization focused on democracy, human rights, and social and economic justice in Latin America.

[38] Washington Office on Latin America, *Transnational Youth Gangs in Central America, Mexico, and the United States*, February 8, 2007.

[39] James C. Spero, U.S. DHS, ICE, testimony before the U.S. House of Representatives, Committee on Government Reform, "MS-13 and Counting: Gang Activity in Northern Virginia," no. 109-194, July 14, 2006.

[40] Ruben Castaneda, "Two MS-13 Members Convicted of Racketeering," *Washington Post*, November 15, 2006, p. B02.

[41] Department of Justice press release, *MS-13 Leader Sentenced to Life in Prison*, September 24, 2007.

[42] Ibid.

[43] Samuel Logan and Ashley Morse, "The Mara Salvatrucha Organization and the U.S. Response," *Power and Interest News Report (PINR)*, January 31, 2007.

[44] See the Illegal Immigration Reform and Immigrant Responsibility Act of 1996 (P.L. 104-208, Division C) and the Anti-Terrorism and Effective Death Penalty Act of 1996 (P.L. 104-132).

[45] See CRS Report RL341 12, *Gangs in Central America.*

[46] Scott Wallace, "You Must Go Home Again: Deported L.A. Gangbangers Takeover El Salvador," *Harper's Magazine*, August 2000.

[47] Diego Cevallos, *Mexico: Spread of Central American Youth Gangs Uncurbed*, Inter Press Service News Agency, Wednesday, June 13, 2007.

[48] U.S. Agency for International Development, Bureau for Latin American and Caribbean Affairs, Office of Regional Sustainable Development, *Central America and Mexico Gang Assessment*, April 2006, pp. 6, 14.

[49] It should be noted that illegal smuggling also occurs at the northern border and that there are reports of MS-13 gang members in Canada; however, the MS-13 presence in Canada is smaller than in Mexico and Central America. See U.S. Department of Homeland Security, Immigration and Customs Enforcement, Office of Inspector General, Office of Audits, *Detention and Removal of Illegal Aliens*, OIG-06-33, April 2006, p. 7.

[50] 18 U.S.C. § 521, added by P.L. 103-322 (the Violent Crime Control and Law Enforcement Act of 1994), Title XV § 150001(a).

[51] The two laws are the Illegal Immigration Reform and Immigrant Responsibility Act (IIRIRA) of 1996 (P.L. 104-208, Division C) and the Anti-terrorism and Effective Death Penalty Act of 1996 (AEDPA, P.L. 104-132). IIRIRA broadly reformed exclusion and deportation procedures. It consolidated exclusion and deportation into a single removal process, expanded the definition of "aggravated felonies" to make more aliens subject to removal, and tightened the standards for relief from removal. AEDPA expanded the class of crimes designated as aggravated felonies, which would subject an alien to expedited removal.

[52] For more information on federal anti-gang grant programs, see CRS Report RL3 3400, *Youth Gangs: Background, Legislation, and Issues*, by Celinda Franco.

[53] For discussion of these initiatives, see CRS Report RL33400, *Youth Gangs: Background, Legislation, and Issues*.

[54] U.S. DOJ, FBI, Headline Archives, *How We're Ganging Up on MS-13*, at http://www.fbi.gov/page2/july05/ms071305.htm, January 22, 2010.

[55] Ibid.

[56] U.S. DOJ, FBI, *The MS-13 Threat: A National Assessment*, at http://www.fbi.gov/page2/jan08/ms13_011408.html, January 21, 2010.

[57] Ibid.

[58] Testimony of FBI Special Agent Grant Ashley, Assistant Director, Criminal Investigative Division, in U.S. Congress, Senate Committee on Judiciary, *Combating Gang Violence in America: Examining Effective Federal, State, and Local Law Enforcement Strategies* (September 17, 2003).

[59] Ibid.
[60] Ibid.
[61] For more information on specific Violent Crime/Gang Task Forces administered by the FBI, see http://www.fbi.gov/ hq/cid/ngic/natgangtfs.htm, January 22, 2010.
[62] *In the Spotlight—Gangs*, U.S. Department of Justice, Office of Justice Programs, National Criminal Justice Reference Service, available at http://www.ncjrs.gov/spotlight/gangs January 22, 2010.
[63] Swecker, FBI testimony, April 20, 2005.
[64] U.S. Congress, House of Representatives, Report 108-792, Making Appropriations for Foreign Operations, Export Financing, and Related Programs for the Fiscal Year Ending September 30, 2005, and For Other Purposes, Conference Report to Accompany H.R. 4818, November 20, 2004, p. 728; U.S. DOJ, FBI, *The MS-13 Threat: A National Assessment*, at http://www.fbi.gov/page2/jan08/ms13_011408.html, January 21, 2010.
[65] U.S. DOJ, ATF, *ATF's Gang Initiatives*, December 2004, p. 50.
[66] More information on PSN is available at http://www.psn.gov/, January 22, 2010.
[67] U.S. DOJ, Press Release, *Attorney General Alberto R. Gonzales Announces Aggressive New Joint Initiatives with El Salvador to Combat Transnational Gangs*, February 5, 2007.
[68] WebWire Internet Press Release Resource, "Three Salvadoran Nationals Indicted on Racketeering Charges for Participation in Violent International Gang," June 6, 2007, available at http://www.webwire.com/ViewPressRel.asp? aId=3 8434, January 22, 2010.
[69] Operation Community Shield has since been expanded to include "all criminal street gangs that pose a threat to national security and public safety." See ICE website, available at http://www.ice.gov/pi/investigations/ comshield/ index.htm, January 22, 2010.
[70] U.S. House, Hearing before the Committee on International Relations Subcommittee on the Western Hemisphere, "Gangs and Crime in Latin America," testimony by John P. Torres, Deputy Assistant Director, Human Smuggling and Public Safety Division, U.S. DHS, April 20, 2005, p. 1.
[71] U.S. DHS, ICE, Protecting National Security and Upholding Public Safety, News Release, *"Paisas" Gang Member Arrested*, May 23, 2007.
[72] U.S. DHS, ICE, "Operation Community Shield," May 22, 2007.
[73] U.S. DHS, CBP, *CBP Today*, "CBP Confronts U.S.'s 'Most Dangerous Gang,' MS-13 Will Commit 'Any Crime at Any Time,'" by Linda Kane, Office of Public Affairs, October/November 2006.
[74] Ibid.
[75] Ibid.
[76] Ibid.
[77] Supported by the Fraternal Order of Police, the National Sheriffs' Association and the National Association of Police Officers, statement by Rep. John Gingery, *Congressional Record*, May 11, 2005, p. H3 120.
[78] Rachel Brand, "Making It a Federal Case: An Inside View of the Pressures to Federalize Crime," Heritage Foundation, Legal Memorandum #30, August 29, 2008, at http://www.heritage.org/Research/LegalIssues/ lm30.cfm#_ftnref1; Paul Rosenzweig, "The Gang Act Needs Modification," Heritage Foundation, WebMemo, May 3, 2004, available at http://www.heritage.org/Research/Crime/wm494.cfm?, January 22, 2010.
[79] Ibid.
[80] For example, see Diverting Children from a Life of Crime: Measuring Costs and Benefits, by Peter W. Greenwood, Karyn E. Model, C. Peter Rydell, and James Chiesa, RAND Corporation, 1996; Three Strikes and You're Out: Estimated Benefits and Costs of California's New Mandatory-Sentencing Law, by Peter W. Greenwood, C. Peter Rydell, Allan F. Abrahamse, Jonathan P. Caulkins, James Chiesa, Karyn E. Model, and Stephen P. Klein, RAND Corporation, December 10, 2005; Justice Policy Institute, Gang Wars: The Failure of Enforcement Tactics and the Need for Effective Public Safety Strategies, "Real Solutions to Youth Violence: Evidence Based Practices," available at http://www.justicepolicy.org/images January 22, 2010; Longitudinal Study: Alternatives to Incarceration Sentencing Evaluation, Year 2, Full Report, State of Connecticut, Judicial Branch, April 1996, pp. 84, 89-91..
[81] Dan M. Kahan, Yale Law School, John M. Olin Center for Studies in Law, Economics, and Public Policy Working Paper Series, *The Logic of Reciprocity: Trust, Collective Action, and Law*, Paper 281, 2002, p. 23.
[82] Ana Arana, "How the Street Gangs Took Central America," *Foreign Affairs*, May/June 2005.
[83] A federal indictment of 30 MS-13 members under existing RICO statutes recently led to the conviction of 3 gang members, who could face sentences of life in prison or the death penalty. According to the superseding indictment of June 4, 2007, the three defendants "conspired to participate in a racketeering enterprise in the United States and El Salvador that involved murder, robbery, obstruction of justice, and witness tampering" as members of MS-13. For more information, see Ruben Castaneda, "Two MS-13 Members Convicted of Racketeering," *Washington Post*, November 15, 2006, p. B02; Ruben Castaneda, "MS-13 Leaders Convicted in Killings," *Washington Post*, April 28, 2007, p. B02, available at http://www.washingtonpost.com/wp-dyn/content/article/2007/04/27/AR2007042702108.html, January 22, 2010; and Jim Kouri, "Two MS-13 Leaders in El Salvador Ordered Gang Killings in the U.S." *American Daily*, June 10, 2007.
[84] California's Street Terrorism Enforcement and Prevention (STEP) law, enacted in 1988, is an often-discussed example of such a law.

[85] See CRS Report R40848, *Immigration Legislation and Issues in the 111th Congress*, coordinated by Andorra Bruno.

[86] The NYGC survey is administered by DOJ's Office of Juvenile Justice and Delinquency Prevention.

[87] Randolph Bourne, "Trans-National America," *Atlantic Monthly*, issue 118, July 1916, pp. 86-97.

In: Transnational Gangs: The MS-13 Gang and Others
Editor: Michele L. Monteith
ISBN: 978-1-61728-917-0

Chapter 2

GANGS IN CENTRAL AMERICA*

Clare Ribando Seelke

SUMMARY

During its second session, the 111th Congress is likely to maintain an interest in the effects of crime and gang violence in Central America, and on the expanding activities of transnational gangs with ties to that region operating in the United States. The violent Mara Salvatrucha (MS-13) and its main rival, the "18th Street" gang (also known as M-18) continue to threaten citizen security and challenge government authority in Central America. Gang-related violence has been particularly acute in Honduras, El Salvador, and Guatemala, which have among the highest homicide rates in the world. Governments in those countries appear to have moved away, at least on a rhetorical level, from repressive anti-gang strategies. However, they have yet to implement effective anti-gang policies that include an emphasis on prevention and rehabilitation of former gang members.

U.S. officials have expressed concerns about the expanding presence of the MS-13 and M-18 in cities across the United States, as well as reports that these gangs may be evolving into more sophisticated transnational criminal enterprises. Between February 2005 and September 2009, U.S. officials arrested some 2,572 alleged MS-13 members in cities across the United States, many of whom were subsequently deported. Evidence suggests, however, that previously deported members of both the MS-13 and the M-18 often reenter the United States illegally across the U.S.-Mexico border.

Several U.S. agencies have been actively engaged on both the law enforcement and preventive side of dealing with Central American gangs. An inter-agency committee worked together to develop a U.S. Strategy to Combat Criminal Gangs from Central America and Mexico, first announced at a July 2007 U.S.-Central American Integration System (SICA) summit on security issues. The strategy, which is now being implemented, states that the U.S.

* This is an edited, reformatted and augmented edition of a United States Congressional Research Service publication, Report RL34112, dated January 11, 2010.

government will pursue coordinated anti-gang activities through five broad areas: diplomacy, repatriation, law enforcement, capacity enhancement, and prevention.

In recent years, Congress has increased funding to support anti-gang efforts in Central America. Congress appropriated roughly $7.9 million in FY2008 and $5 million in FY2009 in global International Narcotics Control and Law Enforcement (INCLE) funds for anti-gang efforts in Central America. Congress provided additional support for anti-gang efforts in the region through the Mérida Initiative, including, by CRS calculation, at least $22 million in FY2008 supplemental assistance and close to $19 million in FY2009 funding. On December 13, 2009, Congress passed the FY20 10 Consolidated Appropriations Act (H.R. 3288/P.L. 111-117), which provides $83 million for combating gangs and drug trafficking in Central America under a new Central America Regional Security Initiative (CARSI). P.L. 111-117 also includes $8 million in global INCLE for gang programs in the region.

This chapter describes the gang problem in Central America, discusses country and regional approaches to deal with the gangs, and analyzes U.S. policy with respect to gangs in Central America. For more information on the Mérida Initiative, see CRS Report R40135, *Mérida Initiative for Mexico and Central America: Funding and Policy Issues*. For information on Central American gangs in the United States, see CRS Report RL34233, *The MS-13 and 18th Street Gangs: Emerging Transnational Gang Threats?*, by Celinda Franco.

INTRODUCTION

In recent years, analysts and U.S. officials have expressed ongoing concerns about the increasing rates of violent crimes committed by drug traffickers, organized criminal groups, and gangs in Central America.[1] U.S. concerns about gangs have accelerated as the Mara Salvatrucha (MS-13), a particularly violent group with ties to Central America, has increased its presence and illicit activities in the United States.[2] Policy-makers in countries throughout the region, including in the United States, are struggling to find the right mix of suppressive and preventive policies to confront the gang problem. Most agree that a comprehensive, regional approach to gangs is necessary to prevent further escalation of the problem.

Congress has maintained an interest in crime and gang violence in Central America, and in the related activities of Central American gangs in the United States.[3] Congress has considered what level of U.S. assistance is most appropriate to help Central American countries combat gang activity and what types of programs are most effective in that effort. Members of Congress have also taken an interest in the effects of U.S. deportations of individuals with criminal records to Central America on the gang problem, as well as the evolving relationship between Mexican drug trafficking organizations and the gangs. Congress has funded anti-gang efforts in Central America through global funds appropriated to the State Department's Bureau of International Narcotics Control and Law Enforcement (INCLE). In June 2008, Congress increased country and regional anti-gang assistance by approving initial funding for the Mérida Initiative, an anti-crime and counterdrug foreign aid package for Mexico and Central America.[4] The 111th Congress appropriated a second tranche of Mérida funding for Central America in the FY2009 Omnibus Appropriations Act (P.L. 111-8), enacted in March 2009. Many Mérida-related programs in Central America are just getting underway after a number of implementation delays.[5]

On December 13, 2009, Congress passed the FY20 10 Consolidated Appropriations Act (H.R. 3288/P.L. 111-117), which includes $83 million for Central America to combat drug trafficking and organized crime, and for judicial reform, institution building, anti-corruption, rule of law, and maritime security. The Act places Central America funding into a new Central America Regional Security Initiative (CARSI), which splits Central America from the Merida Initiative. CARSI funds are subject to the same human rights conditions as those provided in P.L. 111-8.

During its second session, the 111th Congress is likely to exercise oversight over the implementation of the Mérida Initiative and CARSI, with a particular interest in how agencies are coordinating their various anti-gang efforts. Congress may also help influence the design of CARSI as it considers President Obama's FY20 11 budget request.

This chapter describes the gang problem in Central America, discusses country and regional approaches to deal with the gangs, and analyzes U.S. policy with respect to gangs in Central America. It concludes with a discussion of policy issues that Members of Congress may consider as they continue to address aspects of U.S. international anti-gang efforts.

BACKGROUND ON VIOLENT CRIME IN CENTRAL AMERICA

Latin America has among the highest homicide rates in the world, and in recent years homicide rates in several Central American countries have significantly exceeded the regional average (see Table 1). According to figures cited in a recent U.N. Development Program (UNDP) report, Latin America's average homicide rate in 2005 stood at roughly 25 homicides per 100,000 people, almost three times the world average of 9 homicides per 100,000 people.[6] That same year, average homicide rates per 100,000 people in El Salvador, Guatemala and Honduras reached approximately 62, 44, and 37, respectively. Whereas homicide rates in Colombia, historically the most violent country in Latin America, have fallen in the past few years, homicide rates have remained at elevated levels in El Salvador, Guatemala, and, to a lesser extent, Belize. Homicide rates have increased significantly in Honduras. By 2008, the estimated murder rate per 100,000 people stood at roughly 32 in Belize, 52 in El Salvador, 48 in Guatemala, and 58 in Honduras. In Costa Rica, Nicaragua, and Panama, the corresponding figures were 11, 13, and 11, respectively.[7]

Table 1. Estimated Homicide Rates Per 100,000 Inhabitants (2000-2008)

Country	2000	2001	2002	2003	2004	2005	2006	2007	2008
Belize	19	25	30	24	27	28	31	30	32
Costa Rica	6	6	6	7	7	8	8	8	11
El Salvador	45	40	39	40	49	62	65	57	52
Guatemala	28	30	32	37	38	44	47	45	48
Honduras	n/a	n/a	69	65	35	37	46	50	58
Nicaragua	9	10	10	12	12	13	13	13	13
Panama	10	10	12	11	10	11	11	13	19

Source: U.N. Development Program, "Informe Sobre Desarrollo Humano Para América Central 2009-2010: Abrir Espacios a la Seguridad Ciudadana y el Desarrollo Humano," October 2009.

Central America—particularly the "northern triangle" countries of Guatemala, El Salvador, and Honduras—exhibit many risk factors that have been linked to high violent crime rates. For example, studies have shown that high levels of income inequality and social exclusion are often strong predictors of high violent crime rates. Latin America has been among the most unequal in terms of income and levels of social exclusion and most violent regions in the world.[8] This linkage holds true in Central America except for the case of El Salvador, a country with relatively low inequality but high crime rates.[9] With the exceptions of Belize and Costa Rica, Central American countries have also had a long history of armed conflicts and/or dictatorships, which has inhibited the development of democratic institutions and respect for the rule of law. Protracted armed conflicts also resulted in the widespread proliferation of illicit firearms in the region, as well as a cultural tendency to resort to violence as a means of settling disputes. [10] Other traits that make some Central American countries vulnerable to violent crime include highly urbanized populations, growing youth populations, and high unemployment rates. Guatemala, Honduras, and El Salvador, which have large percentages of their populations living in the United States, have reportedly suffered more from the negative effects of emigration (such as family disintegration and deportations) than other countries.[11]

According to the U.N. Office on Drugs and Crime (UNODC), Central American countries are particularly vulnerable to violent crime fueled by drug trafficking and corruption because they are geographically located between the world's largest drug producing and drug consuming countries.[12] In 2008, some 84% of the cocaine shipped from the Andes to the United States flowed through Mexico and Central America. Stepped up enforcement efforts in Mexico has reportedly led traffickers to use Central America as a primary transshipment point for Andean cocaine bound for the United States.[13] Low criminal justice capacity, corruption, and an absence of political will to fight crime in a holistic manner have hindered countries' abilities to respond to violent crime. These problems may be most pronounced in Guatemala, a country struggling, with U.N. assistance, to confront sophisticated organized criminal groups and drug traffickers that have been aligned with some of the country's most powerful political, military, and business actors.[14]

Scope of the Gang Problem in Central America

In recent years, Central American governments, the media, and some analysts have attributed, sometimes erroneously, a significant proportion of violent crime in the region to youth gangs or *maras*, many of which have ties to the United States.

Defining Gangs

Academics and other experts on gangs continue to debate the formal definition of the term "gang" and the types of individuals that should be included in definitions of the term.[15] There is general agreement that most gangs have a name and some sense of identity that can sometimes be indicated by symbols such as clothing, graffiti, and hand signs that are unique to the gang. Gangs are thought to be composed of members ranging in age from 12 to 24, but some gang members are adults well over the age of 24. Typically, gangs have some degree of permanence and organization and are generally involved in delinquent or criminal activity. Gangs may be involved in criminal activities ranging from graffiti, vandalism, petty theft, robbery, and assaults to more serious criminal activities, such as drug trafficking, drug smuggling, money laundering, alien smuggling, extortion, home invasion, murder, and other violent felonies.

Gangs are generally considered to be distinct from organized criminal organizations because they typically lack the hierarchical leadership structure, capital, and manpower required to run a sophisticated criminal enterprise. Gangs are generally more horizontally organized, with lots of small subgroups and no central leadership setting strategy and enforcing discipline. Although some gangs are involved in the street-level distribution of drugs, few gangs or gang members are involved in higher-level criminal drug distribution enterprises run by drug cartels, syndicates, or other sophisticated criminal organizations.

When referring to gangs in Central America, some studies use the term *pandillas* and *maras* interchangeably, while others distinguish between the two.[16] Studies that make a distinction between the two types of Central America gangs generally define *pandillas* as localized groups that have long been present in the region, and *maras* as a more recent phenomenon that has transnational roots.

Transnational Gangs in Central America

The major gangs operating in Central America with ties to the United States are the "18th Street" gang (also known as M-18), and their main rival, the *Mara Salvatrucha* (MS-13).[17] The 18th Street gang was formed by Mexican youth in the Rampart section of Los Angeles in the 1 960s who were not accepted into existing Hispanic gangs. It was the first Hispanic gang to accept members from all races and to recruit members from other states. MS-13 was created during the 1980s by Salvadorans in Los Angeles who had fled the country's civil conflict. Both gangs later expanded their operations to Central America. This process accelerated after the United States began deporting illegal immigrants, many with criminal convictions, back to the region after the passage of the Illegal Immigrant Reform and Immigrant Responsibility Act (IIRIRA) of 1996.[18] Between 2000 and 2004, an estimated 20,000 criminals were sent back to Central America, many of whom had spent time in U.S. prisons for drug and/or gang-related offenses. Many contend that gang-deportees have "exported" a Los Angeles gang culture to Central America and that they have recruited new members from among the local populations. [19]

Estimates of the overall number of gang members in Central America vary widely, but the U.S. Southern Command has placed that figure at around 70,000, a figure also cited by the United Nations. The gang problem is most severe in El Salvador, Honduras, and Guatemala. Estimates of Central American gang membership by country also vary considerably, but UNODC cites country membership totals of some 10,500 in El Salvador, 36,000 in Honduras, and 14,000 in Guatemala. These figures are compared to 4,500 in Nicaragua, 1385 in Panama, and 2,660 in Costa Rica.[20] Nicaragua has a significant number of gang members, but does not have large numbers of MS-13 or M-18 members, perhaps due to the fact that

Nicaragua has had a much lower deportation rate from the United States than the "northern triangle" countries.[21]

While MS-13 and M-18 began as loosely structured street gangs, there is evidence that both gangs, but particularly the MS-13, have expanded geographically and become more organized and sophisticated. By early 2008, for example, Salvadoran police had found evidence suggesting that some MS-13 leaders jailed in El Salvador were ordering retaliatory assassinations of individuals in Northern Virginia, as well as designing plans to unify their *clicas* (cliques) with those in the United States.[22] Studies have shown that, as happened in the United States, gang leaders in Central America are using prisons to recruit new members and to increase the discipline and cohesion among their existing ranks.[23]

Press reports and some current and former Central American officials have blamed MS-13 and other gangs for a large percentage of violent crimes committed in those countries, but some analysts assert that those claims may be exaggerated.[24] Gang experts have argued that, although gangs may be more visible than other criminal groups, gang violence is only one part of a broad spectrum of violence in Central America.[25] In El Salvador, for example, officials have blamed gangs for 60% of all murders committed annually, but UNODC contends that evidence to support that conclusion is lacking. In Guatemala, the regions of the country that have the highest murder rates tend to be those without a significant gang presence, but where organized criminal groups and narco-traffickers are particularly active.[26]

Although the actual percentage of homicides that can be attributed to gangs in Central America remains controversial, the gangs have been involved in a broad array of other criminal activities. Those activities include kidnapping; human trafficking; and drug, auto, and weapons smuggling. Gangs have also been involved in extortions of residents, bus drivers, and business-owners in major cities throughout the region. In San Salvador, for example, gangs regularly demand that citizens pay "war taxes." Failure to pay often results in harassment or violence by gang members.

While some studies maintain that ties between Central American gangs and organized criminal groups have increased, others have downplayed the connection. In recent years, there have been some reports of gang activity in Mexico and along the U.S.-Mexico border. Until Hurricane Stan hit in October 2005, MS-13 members were active in southern Mexico where they often charged migrant smugglers to let their groups pass and sometimes worked in collaboration with Mexican drug cartels. MS-13 members are reportedly being contracted on an ad-hoc basis by Mexico's warring cartels to carry out revenge killings. Regional and U.S. authorities have confirmed increasing gang involvement in drug trafficking and drug-related violence.[27]

Notably, analysts have found no links between Central American gangs and Al Qaeda or other terrorist groups.[28]

Factors Exacerbating the Gang Problem in Central America

Poverty and a Lack of Educational and Employment Opportunities

Several organizations working directly with gang members have asserted that the combination of poverty, social exclusion, and a lack of educational and job opportunities for at-risk youth are perpetuating the gang problem. In Honduras, for example, close to 30% of the population is youth ages 15-24. Those youth have very limited opportunities in a country where some 65% of the population lives on less than $2 a day and the unemployment rate was 25% in 2005. A 2007 World Bank risk assessment for Honduras states that the country has large numbers of unemployed youth who are not in school. Unable to develop the skills required for attending a university or obtaining skilled employment, they provide a ready pool of gang recruits.[29] In the absence of familial and community support, many marginalized youth have turned to gangs for social support, a source of livelihood, and protection.

Societal Stigmas

Societal stigmas against gangs and gang-deportees from the United States have made the process of leaving a gang extremely difficult.[30] A State Department report on youth gangs in El Salvador identifies religious conversion, marriage, enlistment in the military, or enrollment in a substance abuse rehabilitation program as the few options available for those who seek to leave a gang. Many organizations that work with former gang members, particularly those with criminal records, say that offender reentry is a major problem in many countries. Ex-gang members report that employers are often unwilling to hire them. Tattooed former gang members, especially returning deportees from the United States who are often native English speakers, have had the most difficulty finding gainful employment. In El Salvador, several hundred gang members have gone through complete tattoo removal, a long and expensive process, which many feel is necessary to better blend into Salvadoran society.[31]

Role of the Media

Many studies have observed that sensationalist media coverage of the gang phenomenon in Central America has contributed to a sense of insecurity in the region and may have inadvertently enhanced the reputation of the gangs portrayed. For example, a 2006 USAID gangs assessment found that rival gangs in Honduras often compete to see who can portray the most brutal and/or delinquent activities in order to capture the most media attention. Exaggerated media reports may have also contributed to the popular perception, which has been backed by some politicians in Guatemala, Honduras and El Salvador, that youth gangs are responsible for the majority of violent crime in those countries. This sentiment, however erroneous, has led many Central American citizens to support tough law enforcement measures against gangs, hire private security firms, and, in isolated cases, take vigilante action against suspected youth gang members.[32]

Anti-gang Law Enforcement Efforts

While tough law enforcement reforms (discussed below in the section "*Mano Dura*") initially proved to be a way for Central American leaders to show that they were cracking down on gangs, recent studies have cast serious doubts on their effectiveness. In response to law enforcement roundups of any and all tattooed youth, gangs are now changing their behavior to avoid detection. Many gang members are hiding or removing their tattoos, changing their dress, and avoiding the use of hand signals, making them harder to identify and arrest. A regional study concluded that, largely in response to recent law enforcement tactics, gangs have developed into more sophisticated military and business organizations.[33] Those findings are similar to the conclusions of a 2006 regional study which asserted that the repressive policing techniques adopted by many Central American governments may have contributed to gangs "becoming more organized and more violent."[34]

Prisons in Need of Reform

The implementation of aggressive anti-gang roundups has overwhelmed prisons in Central America. Prison conditions in the region are generally harsh, with severe overcrowding, inadequate sanitation, and staffing shortages. Many facilities that were already teeming with inmates have been filled beyond their capacities with thousands of suspected gang members, many of whom have yet to be convicted of any crimes. In El Salvador, for example, as of December 2008, some 19,814 inmates were being held in prisons designed to hold a maximum of 8,227 people.[35]

Due to a lack of security within the prisons, gangs are often able to carry out criminal activities from behind bars, sometimes with assistance from corrupt prison officials. As previously mentioned, there is evidence that gangs have become larger, better organized, and more cohesive within the confines of many of the region's prisons. Some observers have described prisons as "gangland finishing schools"[36] where, rather than being rehabilitated, first-time offenders often deepen their involvement in illicit gang activities.

Disputes between members of rival gangs, between gang and non-gang inmates, and between gangs and prison guards regularly occur. Between January and October 2008, the Honduran Ministry of Security reported 39 inmate deaths, a majority of which occurred as a result of inter- gang violence.[37] Prisoner abuse and torture is also not uncommon.

U.S. Deportations to Central America and the Gang Problem

Policymakers in Central America have expressed ongoing concerns that increasing U.S. deportations of individuals with criminal records is worsening the gang and security problems in the region.[38] The Central American countries of Honduras, Guatemala, and El Salvador have received the highest numbers of U.S. deportations (after Mexico) for the last several fiscal years. Despite the large numbers of deportees repatriated to the region, the Central American countries have typically had a lower percentage of criminal deportees than other top receiving countries (see Table 2). In FY2008, for example, criminal deportees accounted for just 19% of Guatemalans and Hondurans deported. In contrast, criminal deportees accounted for 79% of Jamaican deportees and 55% of Dominican deportees. In FY2009, however, the percentage of Central American deportees with criminal records increased significantly. This may be due to increasing efforts by U.S. Immigration and Customs Enforcement (ICE), in partnership with local and state officials, to identify illegal immigrants subject to deportation.

For the past several years, Central American officials have asked the U.S. government to consider providing a complete criminal history for each criminal deportee, including whether or not he or she is a member of a gang. While ICE does not provide a complete criminal record for deportees, it may provide some information regarding an individual's criminal history when specifying why the individual was removed from the United States. ICE does not indicate gang affiliation unless it is the primary reason why the individual is being deported. However, law enforcement officials in receiving countries are able to contact the

Federal Bureau of Investigation (FBI) in order to request a criminal history check on particular criminal deportees after they have arrived in that country. With support from the Mérida Initiative, ICE and the FBI have developed a pilot program called the Criminal History Information Program (CHIP) to provide more information about deportees with criminal convictions to officials in El Salvador, Honduras, and Guatemala.

The types of support services provided to deportees returning from the United States and other countries vary widely across Latin America. While a few large and relatively wealthy countries (such as Colombia and Mexico) have recently established comprehensive deportee reintegration assistance programs, most countries provide few, if any, services to returning deportees. In Central America, for example, the few programs that do exist tend to be funded and administered by either the Catholic Church, non-governmental organizations (NGOs), or the International Organization for Migration (IOM). The U.S. government does not currently support any deportee reintegration services programs in Central America, although it has in the past.[39]

COUNTRY ANTI-GANG EFFORTS

Country efforts to deal with gangs and gang-related violence has varied significantly. In general, governments in the "northern triangle" countries have adopted more aggressive law enforcement approaches than the other Central American countries. These policies, which will subsequently be discussed, failed to stave off rising crime rates in the region and had several negative unintended consequences. As a result, recent studies maintain that governments appear to be moving away from "enforcement-first" policies towards "second-generation" anti-gang programs. Newer programs have emphasized, among other things, prevention programs for at-risk youth, interventions to encourage youth to leave gangs, and the creation of municipal alliances against crime and violence.[40]

Table 2. U.S. Deportations to Top Receiving Countries: FY2007-FY2009 (Including Annual Percentage of Deportees with Criminal Records)

Country	FY2007	% Crim.	FY2008	% Crim.	FY2009	% Crim.
Mexico	176,815	42.7%	251,875	33.8%	274,577	37.9%
Honduras	30,227	17.6%	29,758	18.8%	27,566	25.1%
Guatemala	26,429	15.3%	28,866	18.5%	30,229	2 1.5%
El Salvador	21,029	24.2%	20,949	27.4%	21,049	30.0%
Dom. Republic	3,709	56.4%	3,776	55.4%	3,824	56.8%
Brazil	3,708	10.0%	3,640	10.7%	3,229	11.7%
Colombia	3,239	37.7%	2,823	39.7%	2,617	42.8%
Ecuador	1,612	27.4%	2,478	23.6%	2,503	25.7%
Nicaragua	2,310	22.7%	2,334	23.4%	2,142	28.6%
Haiti	1,572	34.2%	1,649	25.8%	687	67.8%
Jamaica	1,451	81.2%	1,599	78.9%	1,620	77.3%

Source: Prepared by CRS with information provided by the Department of Homeland Security, Immigration and Customs Enforcement, Office of Detention and Removal. Figures include "removals," but not voluntary returns. FY2009 figures are not yet available.

Mano Dura (Heavy-Handed) Anti-Gang Policies

Mano Dura is a term used to describe the type of anti-gang policies initially put in place in El Salvador, Honduras, and, to a lesser extent, Guatemala in response to popular demands and media pressure for these governments to "do something" about an escalation in gang-related crime. *Mano dura* approaches have typically involved incarcerating large numbers of youth (often those with visible tattoos) for illicit association, and increasing sentences for gang membership and gang-related crimes. A *Mano Dura* law was passed by El Salvador's Congress in 2003, followed by a *Super Mano Dura* package of anti-gang reforms in July 2004. These reforms outlawed gang membership, enhanced police power to search and arrest suspected gang members, and stiffened penalties for convicted gang members. Similarly, in July 2003, Honduras enacted a penal code amendment that made *maras* illegal and established sentences of up to 12 years in prison for gang membership. Changes in legislation have been accompanied by the increasing use of joint military and police patrols to round-up gang suspects. Guatemala introduced similar legislation in 2003, but the legislation never passed. Instead, the Guatemalan government has launched periodic law enforcement operations to round up suspected gang members.

What Have Been the Effects of *Mano Dura* Policies?

Mano Dura reforms initially proved to be a way for Central American leaders to show that they were getting tough on gangs and crime, despite objections from human rights groups about their potential infringements on civil liberties and human rights. Early public reactions to the tough anti-gang reforms enacted in El Salvador and Honduras were extremely positive, supported by media coverage demonizing the activities of tattooed youth gang members. Tony Saca was elected to the presidency of El Salvador largely on the basis of his promises to further crack down on gangs and crime. *Mano Dura* enabled police to arrest large numbers of suspected gang members, including some 14,000 youth in El Salvador between mid 2004 and late 2005. In addition, according to Salvadoran officials, even though many suspects were eventually released, gang detainees provided law enforcement officials with invaluable sources of intelligence information that those officials have since used to design better anti-gang strategies.[41]

Despite the early apparent benefits of *Mano Dura* policies, effects on gangs and crime have been largely disappointing. This may be because a large percentage of violent crime in Central America is not actually gang related. Six years after the implementation of *mano dura* policies, it has become apparent that

- Violent crime remains at extremely elevated levels in El Salvador, Guatemala, and Honduras, making them among the most violent countries in the world.
- Most youth arrested under *mano dura* provisions have been subsequently released for lack of evidence that they committed any crime. Salvadoran police estimated that more than 10,000 of 14,000 suspected gang members arrested in 2005 were later released.[42]

- Some youth who were wrongly arrested for gang involvement have been recruited into the gang life while in prison.
- Gang roundups have exacerbated prison overcrowding and inter-gang violence within the prisons has resulted in several inmate deaths.
- There have been credible reports that extrajudicial youth killings by vigilante groups have continued since *mano dura* went into effect, including alleged assassinations of gang suspects and gang deportees from the United States.
- Finally, in response to *mano dura,* gangs are changing their behavior to avoid detection.

Alternative Approaches

Although their efforts have received considerably less international attention than El Salvador, Honduras and Guatemala, other Central American countries have developed a variety of programs to deal with the gang problem. In Panama, the Ministry of Social Development, in coordination with other government entities and several NGOs, administers gang prevention programs, as well as a program to provide job training and rehabilitation services to former gang members. In 2006, the Inter-American Development Bank (IDB) approved a $22.7 million loan to Panama to fund that and other programs aimed at preventing youth violence in four of the country's largest municipalities. Nicaragua has adopted a national youth crime prevention strategy that, with the active involvement of the police, focuses on family, school, and community interventions. With support from other countries and NGOs, the Nicaraguan National Police's Juvenile Affairs Division runs at least two anti-gang activities a month. The Ministry of the Interior is administering a five-year program, which is supported by funding from the IDB, to target at-risk youth in 11 different municipalities. While less is known about Costa Rica's gang prevention efforts, the country has adopted a prison model based on rehabilitation. As of 2006, some 33% of prisoners in Costa Rica studied and 70% worked, primarily in agriculture.[43]

Prospects for Country Prevention and Rehabilitation Efforts

In the last few years, Central American leaders, including those from the "northern triangle countries, appear to have moved, at least on a rhetorical level, towards more comprehensive anti- gang approaches. In mid-December 2007, then-Salvadoran President Tony Saca opened a summit of the Central America Integration System by stating that the gang problem had shown the importance of coordinated anti-crime efforts, with the most important element of those efforts being prevention.[44] All of the Central American countries have created institutional bodies to design and coordinate crime prevention strategies and have units within their national police forces engaged in prevention efforts. In general, however, government-sponsored gang prevention programs have tended, with some exceptions, to be small-scale, ad-hoc, and underfunded. Governments have been even less involved in sponsoring rehabilitation programs for individuals seeking to leave gangs, with most reintegration programs funded by church groups or NGOs.

Central American government officials have generally cited budgetary limitations and competing concerns, such as drug trafficking, as major factors limiting their ability to implement more extensive prevention and rehabilitation programs. Experts have asserted, however, that it is important for governments to offer educational and job opportunities to youth who are willing to leave gangs before they are tempted to join more sophisticated criminal organizations. It is also critical, they argue, for intervention efforts to focus on strengthening families of at-risk youth.[45]

Research has shown that successful anti-gang efforts involve governments working in close collaboration with civil society, the private sector, churches, mayors, and international donors in order to leverage limited public resources.[46] In fact, many successful anti-gang programs have developed as a result of community-driven efforts to respond to particular problems which are then supported by capacity-building programs for leaders from those communities. Although these types of programs may benefit from financial contributions from local and/or national governments, they may also need non-financial support, including "training, information sharing, leadership, or simply the provision of a dedicated space for programming or meetings."[47]

Regional and Multilateral Efforts

Central American Integration System (SICA)

Some analysts maintain that the emergence of gangs as a regional security threat has led the Central American countries to "engage in unprecedented forms of regional cooperation."[48] For the last several years, Central American leaders and officials have regularly met, often accompanied by their U.S. and Mexican counterparts, to discuss ways to coordinate security and information- sharing on gang members and other criminal groups. Most of these regional security meetings have been organized by the Security Commission of the Central American Integration System (SICA).[49] The leaders of the SICA members states and the President-elect of Mexico began developing a regional security strategy in October 2006, which was subsequently adopted at a summit held in August 2007.[50] The strategy identifies eight threats to regional security, including organized crime, drug trafficking, deportees with criminal records, gangs, homicide, small arms trafficking, terrorism, and corruption. In the strategy, the leaders vow to: designate transnational gang liaison offices in each country that will compile and share information, conduct joint investigations, and establish a regional database on gangs.

Up until this point, however, most regional anti-gang cooperation has occurred on a declarative, rather than an operational level. At least one youth violence prevention project is now being implemented by the Secretariat, based in El Salvador, in cooperation with the U.S. Agency for International Development (USAID).[51] SICA has estimated that the costs to implement its regional security plan could exceed $953 million, including $60 million for anti-gang efforts.[52] Some observers think that more regional anti-gang cooperation is possible, but others predict that political differences among Central American governments and instability in particular countries is likely to inhibit future efforts.

Organization of American States (OAS)

On June 7, 2005, the OAS passed a resolution to hold conferences and workshops on the gang issue and to urge member states to support the creation of holistic solutions to the gang problem. In the past four years, the OAS has hosted meetings and conferences on the gang problem in Latin America and conducted a study on how to define and classify the types of gangs operating in the region. On June 5, 2007 the OAS General Assembly passed a resolution to promote hemispheric cooperation in confronting criminal gangs that instructs the General Assembly to support country anti-gang efforts and the Permanent Council to create a contact group of member states concerned about the gang issue. On January 12, 2008, the OAS Permanent Council held a special session devoted to the problem of criminal gangs.

Inter-American Coalition for the Prevention of Violence (IACPV)

The IACPV is a multilateral group formed in 2000 to promote prevention as a viable way of addressing crime and violence in Latin America. IACPV member organizations include the OAS, World Bank, Pan American Health Organization (PAHO), Inter-American Development Bank (IDB), USAID, Centers for Disease Control and Prevention (CDC), and the United Nations Educational, Scientific, and Cultural Organization (UNESCO). The IACPV has helped municipalities in Central America develop violence prevention plans, developed a user-friendly violence indicators document, hosted a major conference on gang prevention, and provided technical and financial assistance to help form a counterpart organization within the region, the Central American Coalition for the Prevention of Youth Violence.

Multilateral Development Banks and Donor Agencies

The U.N. Development Program (UNDP), the IDB, and the World Bank are some of the multilateral donors involved in supporting violence reduction and anti-gang programs in Central America. UNDP, for its part, has supported small arms control; police reform; violence reduction; and disarmament, demobilization, and reintegration programs in Central America. UNDP has also conducted research projects on the costs of violence in El Salvador, as well as a comprehensive regional study published in October 2009 on security challenges facing Central America. The IDB has executed significant violence reduction loans in El Salvador, Guatemala, Honduras, and Panama. On May 24, 2007, the IDB, in coordination with UNODC and the OAS, hosted a seminar in Washington, DC, on crime and violence in Central America. The World Bank has produced analytical studies, with a particular emphasis on identifying best practices in reducing crime and violence; introduced crime and violence prevention components into existing Bank-funded projects in urban areas; and developed a program to give small grants to community-based violence prevention initiatives.

U.S. POLICY

In recent years, Administration officials and Members of Congress have expressed ongoing concerns about gangs and violence in Central America and their spillover effects on the United States. In September 2009 congressional testimony, FBI Director Robert Mueller stated that "criminal gangs ... are of increasing concern for domestic and international law enforcement ... [and that] the MS-13 [in particular] continues to expand its influence in the United States."[53] U.S. officials are striving to coordinate anti-gang initiatives on both the domestic and international fronts, taking into account their likely impacts on domestic security, on the one hand, and on foreign relations with the countries of Central America and Mexico, on the other.

Congressional Interest

Congress has expressed increasing concern about the problem of transnational gangs and interest in the effectiveness of U.S. international anti-gang efforts. In the 110th Congress, interest in the topic of gangs and violence in Central America included concerns about the unintended consequences of *mano dura* policies, the relationship between gangs and drug cartels, and the effects of U.S. deportation policy on the gang problem. On October 2, 2007, the House passed H.Res. 564 (Engel) supporting expanded cooperation between the United States and Central America to combat crime and violence.

During its first session, the 110th Congress also enacted the FY2008 Consolidated Appropriations Act, P.L. 110-161, which included $7.9 million in global INCLE funding for the State Department Bureau of International Narcotics and Law Enforcement Affairs (INL) anti-gang programs. In October 2007, the Bush Administration proposed the Mérida Initiative, a new anticrime and counterdrug program for Mexico and Central America. During its second session, the 110th Congress considered the proposal, eventually appropriating $60 million for the Central America portion of the Mérida Initiative in the FY2008 Supplemental Appropriations Act, (P.L. 110-252). As compared to the Bush Administration's budget request, Congress shifted the bulk of Mérida funding for anti-gang programs from law enforcement to institution building, rule of law, and development programs.

The 111th Congress appropriated another $5 million in global INCLE funding for INL efforts in Central America, as well as $100 million in Mérida funding for the region in the FY2009 Omnibus Appropriations Act (P.L. 111-8) in March 2009, including $12 million for ESDF programs. For FY20 10, the Obama Administration requested $7 million in global INCLE funds for INL programs in Central America, as well as $100 million for the Central American portion of the Mérida Initiative. On December 13, 2009, Congress passed the FY2010 Consolidated Appropriations Act (H.R. 3288/P.L. 111-117), which includes $83 million for Central America to combat drug trafficking, gangs, and organized crime, and for judicial reform, institution building, anti-corruption, rule of law, and maritime security. The Act places Central America funding into a new Central America Regional Security Initiative (CARSI), which splits Central America from the Merida Initiative. CARSI funds are subject to the same human rights conditions as those provided in P.L. 111-8.

U.S. International Anti-Gang Efforts

For at least the last five years, several U.S. agencies have been actively engaged on both the law enforcement and preventive side of dealing with Central American gangs. In 2004, the FBI created an MS-13 Task Force to improve information-sharing and intelligence-gathering among U.S. and Central American law enforcement officials. In 2005, the Bureau of Immigrations and Customs Enforcement (ICE) within the Department of Homeland Security created a national anti- gang initiative called "Operation Community Shield." In addition to arresting suspected gang members in the United States, ICE began working more closely with its offices overseas to coordinate with foreign governments also experiencing gang problems. Since February 2005, ICE has arrested more than 2,572 suspected MS-13 members in the United States.[54] Also in 2005, the U.S. Agency for International Development (USAID) undertook a comprehensive assessment of the gang problem in Central America and Mexico. In that assessment, USAID found that while a few U.S. programs addressed some aspects of the gang phenomenon, several new initiatives would be needed in the areas of prevention, law enforcement, and rehabilitation/reintegration.

Throughout 2005 and 2006, an inter-agency committee worked together to develop a U.S. Strategy to Combat Criminal Gangs from Central America and Mexico, which was announced at a July 18, 2007 U.S.-SICA summit on security issues.[55] The strategy acknowledged that, based on previous U.S. and regional experiences, future anti-gang efforts should be holistic, comprehensive, and regional in scope. It called for active engagement with governments in the region, the OAS, and the SICA. The strategy stated that the U.S. government will pursue coordinated anti-gang activities in five broad areas: diplomacy, repatriation, law enforcement, capacity enhancement, and prevention. Selected current initiatives by U.S. agencies to implement the international components of that strategy are discussed below.

State Department

Over the last several years, the State Department's INL Bureau has provided training and technical assistance to law enforcement officials throughout Central America, sponsored anti-gang workshops at the International Law Enforcement Academy (ILEA)[56] in San Salvador, and implemented a "model precinct" to improve policing and police-community relations in Villanueva, Guatemala. Some initial funding for these programs came from $16 million in unspent Andean Counterdrug Program funds that were reprogrammed in September 2007 to support INL's drug interdiction operations, anti-gang efforts, and demand reduction initiatives in Central America. Since FY2008, INL programs have also been funded by a line item in the Foreign Operations budget designated for "Criminal Youth Gangs." Funding for this program totaled $7.9 million in FY2008 and an estimated $5 million in FY2009.

In January 2008, INL sent a Regional Gang Advisor to El Salvador to coordinate its Central American gang programs. In July 2008, that Advisor produced a detailed assessment of the gang problem in Honduras, El Salvador, and Guatemala and a work plan focusing on six key areas: investigative capacity, legal capacity, intelligence capacity, community policing, prevention, and prisons. Since that time, the Regional Gang Advisor has initiated country and regional prevention activities, sponsored trainings and technical exchanges for police and prison officers from across the region, taught an ILEA anti-gang course, and identified sites for community policing programs to be established in El Salvador and Honduras.[57]

Additionally, the Department of State, which is charged with coordinating the implementation of the Administration's Mérida Initiative in Central America, has identified gangs as one of the critical threats facing the citizens of Central America, and has allocated resources accordingly to the Department of Justice and the U.S. Agency for International

Development to enable these implementing agencies to counter the impact of gangs in the region.

Department of Justice

Within the Department of Justice (DOJ), the FBI is implementing several programs to improve the capacity of law enforcement in Central America to carry out investigations and share intelligence on gang suspects. The Office of Overseas Prosecutorial Development, Assistance, and Training (OPDAT) has also provided some training on prosecuting gang-related cases to judicial officials in the region. The deployment of a Bureau of Alcohol, Tobacco, Firearms and Explosive (ATF) Regional Advisor to San Salvador will also enable ATF to support transnational gang investigations involving U.S. origin firearms. Many FBI, OPDAT, and ATF programs are supported by the Mérida Initiative or other State Department funding and are carried out in collaboration with INL. Recent programs include

- **Central American Fingerprinting Exploitation (CAFÉ):** a criminal file/fingerprint retrieval initiative that has incorporated more than 72,000 finger prints from gang members from Mexico, El Salvador, Belize, Honduras, and Guatemala into the FBI's Integrated Automated Fingerprint Identification System since 2006. The data are accessible to Central American police officials. FY2009 Mérida funding will be used to expand this program to all countries in the region.
- **Transnational Anti-Gang (TAG) Units:** a program that began in El Salvador in October 2007 involving the creation of vetted police units that work with FBI agents stationed in San Salvador on investigating gang-related cases. TAG activities are being expanded into Guatemala with FY2009 Mérida funding, and further expansion into Honduras is expected to occur once the political situation in that country permits renewed levels of U.S.-Honduran law enforcement cooperation.
- **Central American Law Enforcement Exchange (CALEE):** a joint FBI/INL program that recently began to bring law enforcement officials from Central America together with their counterparts from several large U.S. cities to share information and intelligence.
- **Repatriation-Criminal History Information Program (CHIP):** a joint FBI/ICE, Mérida Initiative-funded program to provide more complete criminal history information on U.S. deportees to Central American law enforcement officials in receiving countries. CHIP will begin in El Salvador in 2010, and then be expanded to Guatemala and Honduras.[58]

USAID

USAID has provided $2.8 million for a regional anti-gang program cosponsored by SICA, known as the "Regional Youth Alliance USAID-SICA." The program, which began in April 2008, involves: 1) the creation of public-private partnerships to support prevention and rehabilitation programs in Guatemala, Honduras, and El Salvador; 2) an assessment of the juvenile justice systems in each of those countries followed by efforts to reform those systems; and, 3) collaborating with SICA to evaluate each of these initiatives and to create and implement new policy responses. As part of its efforts to sponsor community-based programs, the Regional Youth Alliance aims to provide 45 sub-grants to local NGOs in targeted communities, many of which are offering computer-based job training to at-risk youth. Those sub-grants aim to reach some 300 community leaders and 3,000 youth.

USAID is also implementing country and regional anti-gang programs with support from the Mérida Initiative Economic and Social Development Fund (ESDF) for Central America that was created by P.L. 110-252, the FY2008 Supplemental Appropriations Act. With ESDF funding, USAID plans to support Community Action Fund (CAF) activities that provide at-risk youth in high-crime communities with basic or secondary education and job training. CAF activities will be modeled after the Regional Youth Alliance program. USAID will also support Community Crime and Gang Prevention Programs (CCGP) that focus on strengthening the role of local governments in developing citizen security and anti-gang programs. ESDF will also fund community policing activities.

One problem currently being encountered in the region relates to the timely delivery of funds for anti-gang programs. For instance, many Mérida-funded efforts are just getting underway, as FY2008 supplemental funding did not arrive to most of the USAID Missions in Central America until August 2009. Mérida programs in Honduras have yet to begin because of the termination of some USAID assistance to that country in the wake of President Manuel Zelaya's ouster in late June 2009.

Policy Approaches and Concerns

Most policy-makers agree that finding regional solutions to the gang problem is essential. Many also concur that in order to effectively reduce gang-related crime, a holistic approach to the problem must be developed that addresses its root social, political, and economic causes. There is disagreement, however, over the proper level and combination of preventive and suppressive policies that should be used in Central America to address the gang problem and over what U.S. agency is best equipped to oversee those efforts.

Debates regarding the relative merits of prevention and suppression methods reemerged when the 110th Congress considered the Bush Administration's FY2008 supplemental budget request for the Mérida Initiative. As previously mentioned, Congress increased funding for rule of law, prevention, and development programs and reduced funding for some police training and equipment programs as compared to the budget request. It did so by earmarking $25 million in Economic Support Funds (ESF) for the creation of an Economic and Social Development Fund (ESDF) for Central America. Congress also increased the amount of funds appropriated to USAID vis-à-vis INL and other law enforcement agencies by stipulating that of the FY2008 ESF funds provided, $20 million are to be administered by USAID. The 111th Congress included another $12 million for the ESDF in the FY2009 Omnibus Appropriations Act (P.L. 111-8) to support USAID programs in violence-prone communities.

Proponents of law enforcement solutions maintain that Central American law enforcement officials lack the capacity and resources to target gang leaders effectively, share data, and conduct thorough investigations that lead to successful prosecutions. In addition to supporting specialized anti-gang units, the Mérida Initiative seeks to address these issues by providing funding for police training to build investigative capacity and communications equipment for police forces. The Initiative does not include funds to support large-scale police reform, even though corruption within law enforcement is a major obstacle to current anti-gang efforts. It does, however, aim to improve police-community relations, which have been very poor in many communities, through support for community policing programs modeled after the successful U.S.-funded program in Villanueva, Guatemala.

While most U.S. observers argue that the State Department and FBI should take the lead in assistance to improve law enforcement capacity, others see a possible role for the U.S. Southern Command in training regional security forces.[59] In recent years, the U.S. Southern Command has taken a leading role in discussing the problem of citizen security in Central America, both within the U.S. inter-agency community and with Central American officials. Critics of U.S. military involvement in anti-gang efforts have noted that it is the State Department's role to provide security assistance to foreign governments, subject to human rights and democracy concerns. They have expressed satisfaction that the Mérida Initiative emphasizes regional cooperation by civilian agencies on public security issues through the U.S.-SICA dialogue, with no explicit role established for the U.S. Southern Command or the region's militaries.[60]

Based on the experiences of cities throughout the United States, proponents of more prevention- based interventions argue that localities that provide social services to at-risk youth have been more effective in preventing gang violence than those that have relied only on law enforcement approaches.[61] These findings mirror the results of several studies previously cited in this chapter that focus on reducing gang violence in Central America. As a result, human rights groups urged Congress to include more of an emphasis on prevention and rehabilitation in the Mérida Initiative than the Bush Administration had originally proposed.[62] As previously stated, Congress increased funding for prevention programs, as well as economic and social development programs, in the FY2008 Supplemental Appropriations Act (P.L. 110-252) and the FY2009 Omnibus Act (P.L. 111-8).

End Notes

[1] The Central American countries include Belize, Costa Rica, El Salvador, Guatemala, Honduras, Nicaragua, and Panama. This chapter focuses on the "northern triangle" countries of Central America where the gang problem has been most acute, which include El Salvador, Guatemala, and Honduras. It refers to the other countries and governments in the region periodically for comparative purposes.

[2] U.S. Department of Justice (DOJ), National Gang Intelligence Center, "National Gang Threat Assessment (NGTA) 2009," January 2009.

[3] For information on Central American gangs active in the United States, see CRS Report RL34233, *The MS-13 and 18th Street Gangs: Emerging Transnational Gang Threats?*, by Celinda Franco.

[4] For more information on the Mérida Initiative, see CRS Report R40135, *Mérida Initiative for Mexico and Central America: Funding and Policy Issues*, by Clare Ribando Seelke.

[5] U.S. Government Accountability Office (GAO), "Status of Funds for the Mérida Initiative," December 3, 2009, GAO 10-253R, available at: http://www.gao.gov/products/GAO-10-253R.

[6] U.N. Development Program (UNDP), "Informe Sobre Desarrollo Humano Para América Central 2009-20 10: Abrir Espacios a la Seguridad Ciudadana y el Desarrollo Humano," October 2009. This chapter also contains sections on other types of violent crime in Central America, including rape, kidnapping, assault, and domestic violence.

[7] Ibid.

[8] D. Ledermann et al., "Determinants of Crime Rates in Latin America and the World," *World Bank*, October 1998.

[9] UNDP, October 2009.

[10] Facultad Latinoamericana de Ciencias Sociales (FLACSO), *Armas Pequeñas y Livianas: Amenaza a la Seguridad Hemisférica*, 2007.

[11] UNDP, October 2009.

[12] United Nations Office on Drugs and Crime (UNODC), "Crime and Development in Central America: Caught in the Crossfire," May 2007.
[13] Testimony of Mark L. Schneider, Senior Vice President of the International Crisis Group, before the House Subcommittee on the Western Hemisphere hearing on "Assessing U.S. Drug Policy in the Americas," October 15, 2009.
[14] Ivan Briscoe, "A Criminal Bargain: The State and Security in Guatemala," *Fundación Para las Relaciones Internacionales y El Diálogo Exterior*, September 2009.
[15] This section was drawn from CRS Report RL33400, *Youth Gangs: Background, Legislation, and Issues*, by Celinda Franco.
[16] See, for example, Demoscopia S.A., "Maras y Pandillas: Comunidad y Policía en Centroamérica," October 2007, as opposed to Dennis Rodgers et al., "Gangs of Central America: Causes, Costs, and Interventions," *Small Arms Survey* Occasional Paper 23, May 2009.
[17] For the history and evolution of these gangs, see Tom Diaz, *No Boundaries: Transnational Latino Gangs and American Law Enforcement*, Ann Arbor, M.I.: University of Michigan Press, 2009.
[18] IRIRA expanded the categories of illegal immigrants subject to deportation and made it more difficult for immigrants to get relief from removal.
[19] Ana Arana, "How the Street Gangs Took Central America," *Foreign Affairs*, May/June 2005.
[20] Testimony of General Bantz J. Craddock, Commander, U.S. Southern Command, before the Senate Armed Services Committee, March 15, 2005; UNODC, May 2007.
[21] Rodgers et al., 2009.
[22] U.S. Department of State, Bureau of International Narcotics and Law Enforcement Affairs, "Regional Gang Initiative: Assessments and Plan of Action," July 1, 2008.
[23] Demoscopia S.A, 2007.
[24] For example, see Federico Brevé, former Minister of Defense of Honduras, "The Maras: A Menace to the Americas," *Military Review*, July-August 2007.
[25] Testimony of Geoff Thale, Program Director of the Washington Office on Latin America, before the House Committee on Foreign Affairs, Subcommittee on the Western Hemisphere, June 26, 2007.
[26] UNODC, May 2007; Washington Office on Latin America and the Instituto Tecnológico Autónomo de México (ITAM), "Transnational Youth Gangs in Central America, Mexico and the United States," March 2007.
[27] UNDP, October 2009, U.S. Department of State, Bureau of International Narcotics and Law Enforcement Affairs, "International Narcotics Control Strategy Report 2009," March 2009.
[28] Testimony of Chris Swecker, Assistant Director, Criminal Investigation Division, Federal Bureau of Investigation, before the Subcommittee on the Western Hemisphere of the House Committee on International Relations, April 20, 2005. Testimony of David Shirk, Professor and Director of the Trans-Border Institute, before the House Appropriations Subcommittee on Commerce, Justice and Science, and Related Appropriations, March 24, 2009.
[29] Sara Michel, Elizabeth Utting, and Bob Moquin, "Honduras: a Risk Assessment," *World Bank*, February 2007.
[30] Demoscopia S.A, 2007.
[31] U.S. Department of State, Bureau of Democracy, Human Rights and Labor, "Issue Paper: Youth Gang Organizations in El Salvador," June 2007.
[32] Testimony of Lainie Reisman before the House Committee on Foreign Affairs Subcommittee on the Western Hemisphere, June 26, 2007. For more on the politicization of the gang problem, see Lainie Reisman, "Breaking the Vicious Cycle: Respond to Central American Gang Violence," *Sais Review*, Vol. 26, Summer 2006. The State Department Human Rights Reports covering Guatemala and Honduras for 2008 include references to NGO reports that vigilante torture and even killings of youths have continued to occur. NGOs in both countries have asserted that these abuses may have been perpetrated by groups that included current and former members of the security forces.
[33] Demoscopia, S.A., 2007.
[34] "Youth Gangs in Central America," *Washington Office on Latin America*, November 2006.
[35] U.S. Department of State, "Human Rights Report 2009," February 2009.
[36] Arana, 2005.
[37] Ibid.
[38] Kate Joynes et al., "Central America, Mexico and the United States Formulate Shared Strategy to Fight Gang Violence," *Global Insight Daily Analysis*, April 9, 2008.
[39] Testimony of Maureen Achieng, Chief of Mission for the International Organization for Migration (IOM) in Haiti before the House Subcommittee on the Western Hemisphere, July 24, 2007.
[40] Rodgers et al., May 2009.
[41] U.S. Department of State, INL, "Regional Gang Initiative Assessments and Plan of Action," July 1, 2008.
[42] "Most of 14,000 Gang Members Arrested in El Salvador Were Released," *EFE News Service*, December 27, 2005.

[43] Bernardo Kliksberg, "Mitos y Realidades Sobre la Criminalidad en América Latina: Algunas Anotaciones Estratégicas Cómo Enfrentarla y Mejorar la Cohesión Social," Fundación Internacional y para Iberoamérica de Administración y Políticas Públicas," 2007.

[44] "Centroamérica Revisa Estrategias Para Luchar Contra Pandillas," *Agence France Presse*, December 13, 2007.

[45] Kliksberg, 2007.

[46] USAID Gang Assessment, 2006; José Miguel Cruz, *Street Gangs in Central America*, San Salvador: UCA Editors, 2007.

[47] See the section by Caterina Gowis Roman in "Daring to Care: Community-Based Responses to Youth Gang Violence in Central America and Central American Immigrant Communities in the United States, *WOLA*, October 2008.

[48] Ibid.

[49] The Central American Integration System (SICA) is a regional organization with a Secretariat in El Salvador that is comprised by the governments of El Salvador, Guatemala, Nicaragua, Honduras, Belize, and Panama. The Security Commission was created in 1995 to develop and carry out regional security efforts.

[50] A copy of the strategy is available at http://www.state.gov/p/wha/rls/93586.htm.

[51] USAID, "Press Release: USAID-SICA Regional Youth Alliance Offices Inaugurated," April 9, 2008, available at http://www.usaid.gov/sv/pressreleases/2008-009_Inauguration%20of%20USAID-SICA%20Regional%20Youth%20Alliance%20Offices.pdf.

[52] SICA General Secretariat, Fifth Meeting of the Working Group for Drafting Proposals to Finance Central American Security, May 13-14, 2008.

[53] Testimony by Robert Mueller, Director, Federal Bureau of Investigation (FBI), U.S. Department of Justice, before the Senate Judiciary Committee, September 16, 2009.

[54] U.S. Immigration and Customs Enforcement (ICE), "ICE Arrests More Than 1,780 During the Largest-Ever Nationwide Gang Surge," October 16, 2009.

[55] U.S. Department of State, Office of the Spokesman, "Combating Criminal Gangs from Central America and Mexico," July 18, 2007.

[56] The International Law Enforcement Academy (ILEA) based in San Salvador, El Salvador is one of four regional law enforcement training academies funded by the State Department's INL Bureau. The ILEA in San Salvador offers training and technical assistance to law enforcement officials from throughout Latin America. In 2009, the ILEA conducted five anti-gang courses.

[57] U.S. Department of State, INL, "FY20 10 Program and Budget Guide."

[58] FBI Press Release, "United Against MS-13; Our Central American Partnerships," November 10, 2009. For information on Mérida funding for these programs, see U.S. Department of State, FY2008 Supplemental Appropriations Spending Plan: Mexico, Central America, Haiti, and the Dominican Republic, September 9, 2008, and FY2009 Spending Plan: Mexico, Central America, Haiti, and the Dominican Republic, August 13, 2009.

[59] The only military component in the Administration's proposal for Mérida was the $21 million requested in FY2009 to support Enduring Friendship, a Department of Defense program to provide naval equipment to Central American countries so that they can work with the U.S. Coast Guard and Navy on maritime drug interdiction efforts.

[60] U.S. Department of State, Office of Language Services Translating Division, "Not All That is Gold Glitters and Not All That Glitters is Gold," by Joel Fyke and Maureen Myer, March 2008, originally published in *Foreign Affairs en Español,* Vol. 8, No. 1.

[61] "Gang Wars," *Justice Policy Institute*, Washington, DC, July 2007.

[62] "Memo: The Merida Initiative and Citizen Security in Mexico and Central America," *Washington Office on Latin America*, March 2008.

In: Transnational Gangs: The MS-13 Gang and Others
Editor: Michele L. Monteith
ISBN: 978-1-61728-917-0

Chapter 3

COMBATING GANGS: FEDERAL AGENCIES HAVE IMPLEMENTED A CENTRAL AMERICAN GANG STRATEGY, BUT COULD STRENGTHEN OVERSIGHT AND MEASUREMENT OF EFFORTS*

United States Government Accountability Office

WHY GAO DID THIS STUDY

Thousands of gang members in the United States belong to gangs such as MS-13 and 18th Street that are also active in Central American countries. Federal entities with responsibilities for addressing Central American gangs include the National Security Council (NSC); the Departments of Homeland Security (DHS), Justice (DOJ), and State; and the U.S. Agency for International Development (USAID). GAO was asked to review federal efforts to combat transnational gangs. This chapter addresses (1) the extent to which the federal government has developed a strategy to combat these gangs, and (2) how federal agencies have implemented the strategy and other programs to combat these gangs, coordinated their actions, and assessed their results. GAO examined federal agencies' antigang plans, resources, and measures; interviewed federal, state, and local officials in seven localities representing varying population sizes and geographic regions; and interviewed U.S. and foreign officials in El Salvador and Guatemala where U.S. agencies have implemented antigang programs. The results of these interviews are not generalizable.

* This is an edited, reformatted and augmented edition of a United States Government Accountability Office publication, Report GAO-10-395, dated April 2010.

WHAT GAO RECOMMENDS

GAO recommends that the NSC revise the antigang strategy to include an approach for oversight and performance measures and that DOJ and DHS reach agreement on the composition of an antigang unit in El Salvador. The NSC did not comment. DOJ and DHS agreed with our recommendation to them.

WHAT GAO FOUND

The NSC, in conjunction with State, DOJ, DHS, and USAID, developed a strategy to combat gangs with connections to Central America; however, the strategy lacks an approach or framework to oversee implementation and performance goals and measures to assess progress. GAO previously reported that characteristics such as defining the problem to be addressed as well as the scope and methodology of the strategy; describing agencies' activities, roles, and responsibilities; providing an approach to oversee implementation; and establishing performance measures, among other characteristics, can enhance a strategy's effectiveness. While the antigang strategy contains some of these characteristics, such as identifying the problems and risks associated with the gangs, describing the scope and purpose of the strategy, and defining roles and responsibilities of federal agencies as well as specific implementation activities, it lacks other characteristics such as an approach for overseeing implementation and goals and measures for assessing progress. For example, although agencies coordinate the strategy's implementation through an interagency task force, agency officials reported that this task force does not oversee the strategy's implementation and that no entity exercises oversight responsibility for the strategy's implementation. Similarly, while State and USAID are developing measures to assess the outcomes of their antigang programs, these measures do not encompass all programs under the strategy or track results of the strategy as a whole. Incorporating these characteristics could enhance the accountability of agencies to implement the strategy and provide a means for assessing progress.

To carry out the strategy and combat transnational gangs, federal agencies have implemented programs and taken steps to coordinate their actions and develop performance measures to assess results of individual programs; but, coordination could be strengthened in an antigang unit in El Salvador by reaching agreement on Immigration and Customs Enforcement's (ICE) role in the unit, the only such unit currently in Central America. Agencies use various interagency groups to coordinate with each other, such as DOJ's Anti-gang Coordination Committee. However, improved coordination at the FBI- initiated antigang unit in El Salvador could enhance information sharing. While the FBI requests information directly from Salvadoran police, ICE requests go to its country attaché, then to FBI agents at the unit who pass it on to Salvadoran police, as ICE does not have an agent at the unit. Prior GAO work has shown that agencies should facilitate information sharing and look for opportunities to leverage resources. Although FBI and ICE officials agree that the process could be improved by posting an ICE agent at the unit and have been discussing the possibility since 2008, they have not yet reached agreement on ICE's role. By reaching agreement, the FBI and ICE could strengthen coordination and information sharing. While agencies have established measures to assess programs, as some of the programs are just starting, data collection for many measures is in the early stages.

Abbreviations

ATF	Bureau of Alcohol, Tobacco, Firearms, and Explosives
BOP	Federal Bureau of Prisons
CARSI	Central American Regional Security Initiative
CBP	U.S. Customs and Border Protection
DEA	Drug Enforcement Administration
DHS	Department of Homeland Security
DOD	Department of Defense
DOJ	Department of Justice
EOUSA	Executive Office for U.S. Attorneys
FBI	Federal Bureau of Investigation
GangTECC	National Gang Targeting, Enforcement, and Coordination Center
ICE	U.S. Immigration and Customs Enforcement
INTERPOL	International Criminal Police Organization
IOCPCC	International Organized Crime Policy Coordinating Committee
MS-13	Mara Salvatrucha
NDIC	National Drug Intelligence Center
NGIC	National Gang Intelligence Center
NSC	National Security Council
OMG	outlaw motorcycle gang
SOUTHCOM	U.S. Southern Command
State	Department of State
the Strategy	Strategy to Combat the Threat of Criminal Gangs from Central America and Mexico
TAG	Transnational Anti-Gang unit
Treasury	Department of the Treasury
USAID	U.S. Agency for International Development
USAO	U.S. Attorneys' Offices
USMS	U.S. Marshals Service

April 23, 2010

The Honorable Lamar S. Smith
Ranking Member
Committee on the Judiciary
House of Representatives

The Honorable Dianne Feinstein
United States Senate

According to the 2009 National Gang Threat Assessment by the National Gang Intelligence Center (NGIC) and National Drug Intelligence Center (NDIC), as of September 2008, there were approximately 1 million gang members in the United States—a 25 percent increase over 2005 membership levels.[1] The assessment found that street gangs that operate throughout most of the United States are a significant threat that has become magnified as national- and regional-level street gangs migrate from urban areas to suburban and rural communities. According to the assessment, gang members engage in a host of criminal activities such as homicide, extortion, drug distribution, and other crimes. Gangs such as the Latin Kings, the Jamaican Posse, Mara Salvatrucha (MS-13), and 18th Street, as well as outlaw motorcycle gangs like the Hells Angels, have been identified by federal law enforcement officials as transnational gangs— gangs whose members are present in and criminally active in more than one country. Of these, gangs with ties to Central America such as MS-13 and 18th Street have been specifically identified as posing serious threats to the public safety of communities in the United States and in Central American countries due to their extremely violent nature, the breadth of their criminal activities, and their rapid expansion.[2] Our report focuses primarily on U.S. federal agencies' efforts to combat these gangs with ties to Central America.

A wide variety of federal departments and agencies have responsibilities for addressing the issue of gangs with ties to Central America, including the Departments of Justice (DOJ), Homeland Security (DHS), State (State), and Defense (DOD), and the U.S. Agency for International Development (USAID). Under the auspices of the National Security Council's (NSC) International Organized Crime Policy Coordinating Committee (IOCPCC),[3] these departments and agencies have collaboratively developed an interagency strategy to combat the threat of criminal gangs with connections to Central America and Mexico. In addition, these departments and agencies work together and with Central American countries and nongovernmental organizations to, among other things, exchange information for use in investigating gang crime, remove gang members who are illegally residing in the United States, and support programs to help prevent young people from becoming gang members or to intervene to provide at-risk youth with alternatives to being part of a gang. In July 2009 we reported on federal efforts to combat gang crime within the United States and coordination mechanisms among federal, state, and local agencies for domestic-based antigang efforts.[4] We discuss the status of our July 2009 recommendations relevant to transnational gangs later in this chapter.

You asked us to examine the extent to which U.S. federal agencies have taken steps to address the problem of transnational gangs. This chapter focuses on U.S. federal agencies' efforts to combat Central American gangs, addressing the following questions: (1) To what extent has the U.S. federal government developed a strategy to combat transnational gangs with connections to Central America? and (2) How have U.S. federal agencies implemented this strategy and related programs to combat transnational gangs with connections to Central America, and to what extent have federal agencies coordinated these programs and assessed their results? In addition, we provide information on the leadership structure and transnational criminal activities of MS-13 and 18th Street (see app. I) and other U.S. gangs that federal law enforcement agencies have identified as having transnational connections (see app. II). We also provide additional details on federal programs for combating transnational gangs (see app. III) and federal antigang coordinating mechanisms and entities (see app. IV).

To determine to what extent the U.S. federal government has developed a strategy to combat transnational gangs with connections to Central America, we examined the interagency strategy developed by various federal departments and agencies under the auspices of the NSC, called the Strategy to Combat the Threat of Criminal Gangs from Central America and Mexico (the Strategy), and compared the contents of the strategy to select criteria in our prior work on desirable characteristics of an effective national strategy, including (1) clear purpose, scope, and methodology; (2) discussion of problems, risks, and threats; (3) desired goals, objectives, activities, and performance measures; and (4) delineation of roles and responsibilities.[5] We also examined the roles and activities of the various federal departments and agencies under the Strategy, including DOJ, DHS, State, DOD, the Department of the Treasury (Treasury), and USAID, and their component agencies, such as the Federal Bureau of Investigation (FBI) within DOJ and U.S. Immigration and Customs Enforcement (ICE) within DHS, that are responsible for carrying out efforts under the Strategy. In regard to the NSC, we discussed its role in developing and implementing the Strategy with a mix of the departments and agencies that participated in the NSC's IOCPCC such as State, DOJ, and USAID.

To determine how U.S. federal agencies have implemented programs to carry out the Strategy and combat transnational gangs, coordinated these programs and assessed their results, we examined a mix of DOJ's, DHS's, State's, USAID's, and their component agencies' plans, performance data, reports, and assessments for fiscal years 2006 through 2009. We compared federal agencies' efforts to coordinate and share information on their transnational antigang programs to select criteria on effective interagency collaboration and results-oriented government.[6] In addition, we reviewed federal agencies' budget requests for fiscal years 2008 through 2010; appropriations acts for DOJ, DHS, State, and USAID and supplemental appropriations acts for those fiscal years; and expenditure plans for U.S. provision of antigang assistance to countries in Central America. To assess the reliability of statistical information, such as data on performance and outcomes, we discussed the sources of the data with agency officials and reviewed documentation regarding the compilation of data. We determined that the data were sufficiently reliable for the purposes of this chapter. To obtain information on federal efforts to combat the gangs as well as the extent to which agencies have coordinated their efforts with other agencies, we interviewed a mix of federal, state, and local law enforcement officials in seven locations in the United States as well as a mix of officials from U.S. federal, foreign, and three nongovernmental agencies in El Salvador and Guatemala. The locations we selected were based on a mix of criteria that included locations (1) along the U.S. borders; (2) where U.S. federal agencies have implemented antigang programs; and (3) where federal law enforcement agencies have conducted operations involving gangs with connections to Central America. For our site visits to foreign locations, we consulted with officials of federal agencies to identify in which foreign locations their agencies had efforts underway. Of the countries in the region, agency officials suggested we visit El Salvador and Guatemala because more antigang initiatives were underway and further along compared to efforts in other countries. Given this, we selected these countries to obtain more information on these efforts and evaluate the effect they have had on the gang problem. To obtain information on the process of how ICE handles and removes gang members who are in the United States illegally, we visited ICE's South Texas Detention Facility in Pearsall, Texas, and interviewed officials with ICE's Office of Detention and Removal Operations. We also observed activities related to gang prevention efforts in El Salvador and Guatemala, such as those at the youth centers, and interviewed participants, local government officials involved in the efforts, and members of the community about their views of the programs and the programs' effect. The information we obtained from interviewing officials in the U.S. and Central American locations cannot be generalized across all locations in the United States or Central America. However, because we selected these locations based on a variety of factors, they provided us with an overview of the agencies' antigang programs, examples of coordination and measurements to assess results, and any challenges with implementation of the programs. Additional details on our scope and methodology, including the locations we visited, are in appendix V.

We conducted this performance audit from April 2008 through April 2010, in accordance with generally accepted government auditing standards. Those standards require that we plan and perform the audit to obtain sufficient, appropriate evidence to provide a reasonable basis for our findings and conclusions based on our audit objectives. We believe that the evidence obtained provides a reasonable basis for our findings and conclusions based on our audit objectives.

BACKGROUND

Overview of Gangs with Connections to Central America

Both the MS-13 and 18th Street gangs were formed in Los Angeles, California. MS-13 was founded by Salvadoran immigrants, many of whom came to the United States to escape the civil war in their native country in the 1980s. The 18th Street gang was founded primarily by Mexican immigrants in the 1960s, though it currently accepts members from other backgrounds. MS-13's early membership is reported to have included former guerrillas and Salvadoran government soldiers whose combat experience during the Salvadoran civil war contributed to the growth of the gang's notoriety as one of the more violent Los Angeles street gangs. The end of the Central American civil wars and changes in U.S. immigration laws helped to facilitate the removal of tens of thousands of Central Americans illegally in the United States to their native countries in the 1990s, including MS-13 and 18th Street gang members who subsequently spread their gang culture and operations to those countries.[7] MS-13 and 18th Street gang members removed from the United States to Central American countries established gangs in those countries.

Within the United States, NGIC has reported that MS-13 has between 8,000 and 10,000 members nationally. The FBI has reported that MS-13 operates in at least 42 states and the District of Columbia. Traditionally, in the United States, MS-13 has consisted of loosely affiliated groups; however, law enforcement officials have reported the coordination of criminal activity among MS-13 gang members operating in the Atlanta, Dallas, Los Angeles, New York, and Washington, D.C., metropolitan areas. In the 2009 National Gang Threat Assessment, the NGIC and NDIC indicated that MS-13 members have been involved in a wide range of crimes within U.S. communities, including homicide, drive-by shootings, assault, robbery, weapons trafficking, the transportation and distribution of drugs, identity theft, and prostitution operations. The 18th Street gang is active in 28 states and has a membership estimated at between 30,000 and 50,000. According to the 2009 National Gang

Threat Assessment, in California, for example, about 80 percent of 18th Street gang members are illegal aliens from Mexico and Central America. In the United States, 18th Street gang members have been involved in homicide, assault, robbery, street-level drug distribution, auto theft, and identification fraud.

Although estimates vary, in the Central American countries of El Salvador, Honduras, Nicaragua, and Guatemala, USAID has estimated that there are approximately 63,000 gang members,[8] while the U.S. Southern Command (SOUTHCOM) has estimated total gang membership in Central America to be approximately 70,000.[9] According to USAID, the majority of these members belong to MS-13 and 18th Street. Within Central American countries, these gangs engage in a range of criminal and violent acts, including homicide, kidnapping, drug smuggling, and extortion, among other crimes.

Overview of Federal Agencies' Missions and Roles in Combating Transnational Gangs

The NSC is the President's principal forum for considering national security and foreign policy matters with his senior national security advisors and cabinet officials. The council also serves as the President's principal arm for coordinating these policies among various government agencies. As such, under its IOCPCC, the NSC coordinated with other federal departments and agencies to develop a strategy to combat the threat of criminal gangs from Central America.

Various other federal departments and agencies play key roles in U.S. federal government efforts to address transnational gangs. As shown in figure 1, these departments include DOJ, DHS, State, USAID, and DOD.

DOJ Component Agencies' Roles and Responsibilities for Combating Transnational Gangs

Within DOJ, seven components have key roles in law enforcement efforts to combat transnational gangs—the Criminal Division; the 93 U.S. Attorneys in 94 judicial districts across the nation that operate with administrative and operational support from the Executive Office for U.S. Attorneys (EOUSA); and four law enforcement agencies—the FBI; Bureau of Alcohol, Tobacco, Firearms, and Explosives (ATF); Drug Enforcement Administration (DEA); and U.S. National Central Bureau of Interpol.[10] The Criminal Division, along with the U.S. Attorneys, is charged with enforcing most federal criminal laws and can prosecute a wide range of criminal matters, including those involving transnational gangs and gang members.[11] The Criminal Division's International Criminal Investigative Training Assistance Program[12] and Office of Overseas Prosecutorial Development, Assistance and Training[13] have been involved in providing antigang training for law enforcement officials and prosecutors from Central America. Also part of the Criminal Division is the Gang Unit, a specialized group of prosecutors charged with developing and implementing strategies to address gangs. In addition to prosecuting gang cases, the Gang Unit prosecutors assist U.S. Attorneys on legal issues and multidistrict cases, as well as work with domestic and foreign law enforcement to coordinate enforcement strategies. The 93 U.S. Attorneys prosecute the majority of criminal cases as well as civil litigation handled by DOJ. EOUSA provides general executive assistance and guidance to U.S. Attorneys' Offices (USAO) and has a national gang coordinator who acts as a liaison between the USAOs and other DOJ components involved in gang prosecution efforts.[14] The FBI's transnational gang efforts target violent crime and criminal enterprises associated with transnational gangs. ATF's primary involvement with MS-13 and 18th Street is related to gang members' illegal possession of, or trafficking in, firearms. DEA targets gangs in connection with specific drug sources or large-scale suppliers who distribute illicit drugs to the gangs. The U.S. National Central Bureau of Interpol is the point of contact for all International Criminal Police Organization (INTERPOL) matters in the United States, including secure communications with police authorities in INTERPOL member countries.[15] As such, among other things, the National Central Bureau receives and sends out notices to INTERPOL bureaus in other countries concerning information or the location of gang members or suspects involved in gang activities.

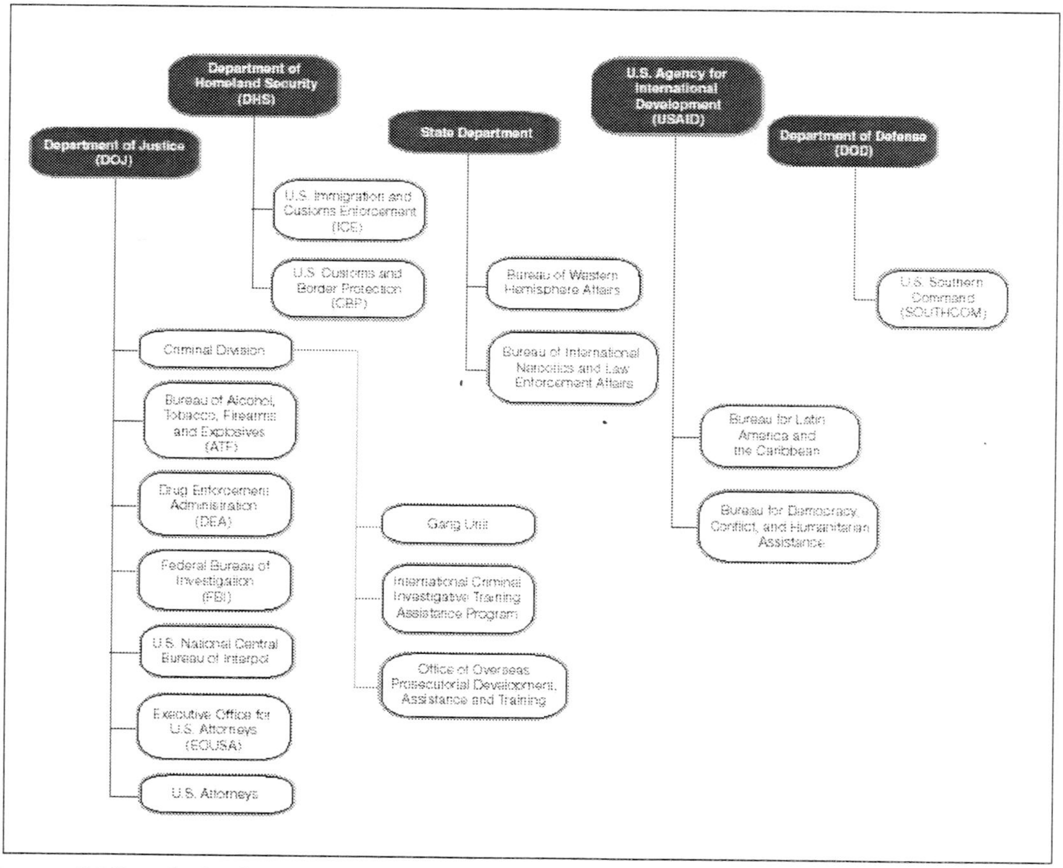

Source: GAO analysis of DOJ, DHS, State, USAID, and DOD information.

Figure 1. Federal Departments and Agencies with Key Roles in Combating Transnational Gangs

DHS Component Agencies' Roles and Responsibilities for Combating Transnational Gangs

Within DHS, ICE's Office of Investigations has a National Gang Unit that manages and coordinates national efforts to combat the growth and proliferation of transnational criminal street gangs. Gang members who are involved in crimes with a nexus to the border, or are foreign-born and are in the United States illegally may be subject to ICE's dual criminal and administrative authorities that are used to disrupt and dismantle transnational gang activities with criminal prosecutions and removal from the United States. In addition, U.S. Customs and Border Protection (CBP), the DHS component that protects U.S. borders against terrorism, illegal immigration, and drug smuggling, among other threats, has a role in identifying gang members at the borders. Upon the arrest of a suspected gang member, CBP will contact ICE and determine if enforcement action is to be taken by CBP or ICE based upon whether the apprehension took place between the ports of entry or at a port of entry. CBP has developed an Anti-Gang Initiative to improve the agency's awareness of gangs through increased partnerships with other federal agencies and to provide gang awareness training for its personnel.

State and USAID Bureaus' Roles and Responsibilities for Combating Transnational Gangs

Two State bureaus, the Bureau of Western Hemisphere Affairs and the Bureau of International Narcotics and Law Enforcement Affairs, are involved in efforts to address gang violence in Central America. The Bureau of Western Hemisphere Affairs is responsible for managing and promoting U.S. interests in the region and fostering cooperation on issues such as drug trafficking and crime. The Bureau of International Narcotics and Law Enforcement Affairs advises the U.S. government on the development of policies and programs to combat narcotics and crime, and works with host nations to strengthen their capabilities so that they can bolster their own effectiveness in fighting drug trafficking and crime including transnational gangs.

USAID provides economic, development, and humanitarian assistance to other countries and, with respect to transnational gangs, is the primary agency responsible for managing gang intervention and prevention efforts in Central America.[16] These efforts are carried out principally through the agency's Bureau for Latin America and the Caribbean and missions in Central America, with technical assistance and support from the Democracy and Governance Office of the Bureau for Democracy, Conflict and Humanitarian Assistance. The agency works with foreign governments and local communities in Central America to support and implement a broad range of programs focused on, among other things, creating employment opportunities and alternatives to participating in gangs.

DOD Roles and Responsibilities for Combating Transnational Gangs

DOD, and specifically SOUTHCOM, has tracked the growth of the gangs in the Central American countries that are within its area of responsibility. Although SOUTHCOM does not have any specific programs in place in Central America to combat transnational gangs, it monitors information on gangs that either pose a threat to the sovereignty of governments in the region or are involved in drug trafficking.

The Mérida Initiative

U.S.-sponsored antigang programs in Central America are being funded in part by the Mérida Initiative. This initiative was announced by the Bush Administration in October 2007 as a multinational effort to confront criminal organizations whose actions affect Mexico, Central America, and the Caribbean countries of the Dominican Republic and Haiti, and spill over into the United States.[17] Through this initiative, the U.S. federal government is providing equipment, training, and other assistance to help these countries address drug and arms trafficking, bulk cash smuggling, and other crime issues such as gangs and organized crime.[18] For Central America, funding under the Mérida Initiative is administered by State and has been allocated to various areas and efforts, including to combat transnational gangs, improve Central American countries' judicial systems, enhance airport and border security in the region, refurbish patrol boats used by Central American countries for intercepting drug traffickers in coastal waters, and a broad range of crime prevention programs, including programs directed at youth at-risk. In fiscal year 2008, the Supplemental Appropriations Act appropriated $60 million for the Central American portion of the Mérida Initiative.[19] In fiscal year 2009, the 2009 Omnibus Appropriations Act appropriated $105 million for Mérida Initiative activities in Central America.[20] Up to $83 million was appropriated for Mérida Initiative activities in Central America for fiscal year 2010 by the Consolidated Appropriations Act, 2010.[21] We recently completed work looking at the status of funds for the initiative and have work ongoing examining U.S. counternarcotics and anticrime assistance provided to Mexico under the initiative.[22] We plan to issue a report on this work later this year.

As of February 2010, federal agencies were developing a strategy for a regional security initiative in Central America, called the Central American Regional Security Initiative (CARSI). This new initiative is in accordance with direction in the conference report accompanying the Consolidated Appropriations Act, 2010, which removed the Central American portion from the Mérida Initiative and placed funding for Central American programs into the new CARSI.[23] Under this new initiative, Central American programs initially funded by the Mérida Initiative, including antigang programs under the Strategy, would be subsumed into CARSI. According to officials from State and USAID, the CARSI strategy is still under development and officials did not have an estimate as to when it would be completed.

In addition to funding provided under the Mérida Initiative, federal agencies have used funding from their operating accounts to implement antigang programs in Central America and the United States. For example, in fiscal years 2007 and 2008 the FBI funded $200,000 and $965,000 from its operating account for establishment of the Transnational Anti-Gang (TAG) unit in El Salvador and the operations of the MS-13 National Gang Task Force, an FBI task force that coordinates FBI-led investigations of MS-13 and 18th Street gangs, respectively. Further, ICE uses funding to conduct transnational gang investigations in the United States and abroad. According to ICE officials, $20.4 million that Congress directed to be used for ICE's antigang activities in fiscal year 2008 funded 119 positions to expand ICE's efforts to combat transnational street gangs.[24] Additionally, USAID officials reported starting their gang prevention programs before Mérida Initiative funding became available and have used non-initiative resources to promote antigang and rule-of-law programs in Central America.

THE INTERAGENCY ANTIGANG STRATEGY CLARIFIES ROLES AND SPECIFIES AGENCY ACTIVITIES, BUT LACKS AN APPROACH FOR OVERSIGHT AND COMPREHENSIVE MEASURES TO ASSESS IMPLEMENTATION EFFORTS

Various federal departments and agencies under the auspices of the NSC developed an interagency strategy for combating gangs with connections to Central America that defines the roles and responsibilities of federal agencies in carrying out the strategy, identifies the problems and risks associated with the gangs, defines its scope and purpose, and identifies specific activities to be taken to achieve results. However, it lacks other key characteristics, such as providing an approach or framework to include an entity for overseeing implementation, and goals and measures for assessing progress and performance in implementing the strategy.

The Antigang Strategy Identifies Roles, Responsibilities, and Activities for Federal Agencies in Combating Transnational Gangs

To respond to the threats criminal gangs such as MS-13 and 18th Street pose to the countries in which they operate, U.S. federal agencies developed the Strategy to Combat the Threat of Criminal Gangs from Central America and Mexico (the Strategy). Issued in July 2007,[25] this interagency strategy was developed under the auspices of the NSC's IOCPCC, comprised of representatives from various federal agencies, including State, DOJ, DHS, USAID, and DOD.[26] The Strategy is designed to combat the threat posed by gangs with links to Central America and Mexico by adopting an approach that integrates law enforcement with youth crime prevention and interventions that provide alternatives to gangs. The Strategy is also designed to be regional in scope, with the United States working with the other countries affected by the gangs to avoid transferring the gang problem to neighboring countries. To implement this approach, the Strategy includes five broad categories under which federal agencies are to take actions to combat transnational gangs—diplomacy, repatriation, law enforcement, capacity enhancement, and prevention—and identifies the activities for agencies to implement under each of these categories. As shown in table 1, for each category, the Strategy identifies agencies that are to implement the individual activities and a lead agency to coordinate these activities. Specifically, the Strategy identifies State as the lead agency for the diplomacy category and, along with USAID, the lead agency for the capacity enhancement category; DHS as the lead agency for the repatriation category and, along with

DOJ, the lead agency for the law enforcement category; and USAID as the lead agency for the prevention category.

Table 1. Categories Related to the Strategy to Combat the Threat of Criminal Gangs from Central America and Mexico and Corresponding Implementing Agencies

Strategy category and description	Lead agency for the category	Example of activities identified under each category	Agency responsible for the activity
Diplomacy: Carry out diplomatic efforts with affected countries to establish a coordinated and comprehensive approach to the gang problem.	State	Work with multilateral organizations, including the Central American Integration System and the Organization of American States, to coordinate and support a regional strategy	State and USAID
		Pursue a policy of engagement with target countries, working with them to identify the best initiatives to pursue at any given time	State and USAID
Repatriation: Expedite the repatriation (removal) process of gang members and provide receiving countries with criminal history information of the gang members.	DHS	Expand the Electronic Travel Document[a] system to countries in the region as conditions permit	DHS
		Provide receiving countries with related information that could help facilitate the reintegration of individuals removed from the United States	DOJ and DHS
Law enforcement: Identify and exploit the gangs' vulnerabilities in order to disrupt their criminal activities and dismantle their criminal infrastructure.	DOJ and DHS	Develop effective channels for sharing intelligence and operational enforcement information pertinent to antigang activities	DOJ and DHS
		Deter and deny, through bilateral and multilateral law enforcement activities, the ability of criminal gangs to engage in transnational criminal activities or recruit new members	DOJ and DHS
Capacity enhancement: Strengthen the capacity of criminal justice systems in Central America and Mexico to identify, prosecute, and incarcerate gang leaders	State and USAID	Provide training and technical assistance to selected elements within the justice system in each country and support the development of regular channels of communication and cooperation among them	DOJ, DHS, State, and USAID

Table 1. (Continued)

Strategy category and description	Lead agency for the category	Example of activities identified under each category	Agency responsible for the activity
and operatives, as well as seize and have them forfeit their assets.		Support community efforts to combat gang crime and violence in the region, including collaboration between law enforcement entities and communities	State, USAID, and DOJ
Prevention: Strengthen the capacity of governments, nongovernmental organizations, and communities to reduce gang activity by discouraging youth from joining gangs and providing rehabilitation and integration options for youth who leave gangs.	USAID	Support efforts to provide rehabilitation and reintegration programs and services to individuals removed from the United States to prevent them from joining a criminal gang or continuing involvement with criminal gangs upon return	USAID, State, DOJ, and DHS
		Assist community-based organizations and local authorities to provide youth with productive alternatives to criminal gang activity or encourage them to leave gangs (e.g., job placement, vocational skills training / alternative education, drug rehabilitation)	USAID and DOJ

Source: Department of State.

Notes: Data are from the Strategy to Combat the Threat of Criminal Gangs from Central America and Mexico.

[a]Under the Electronic Travel Document system, ICE electronically sends travel document applications to the consular officials of these countries who can then electronically sign and certify the documents stating that the countries will receive the illegal aliens to be removed. These documents are also available to ICE electronically. This program eliminates the need for consular officials to visit in person the individual awaiting removal from the United States before issuing documents, helping to reduce the amount of time it takes for ICE to receive travel documents from foreign countries and ultimately remove illegal aliens. The system has been implemented in El Salvador, Guatemala, and Honduras.

As part of our prior work on desirable characteristics of effective national strategies, we have reported that such strategies are the foundation for defining what agencies seek to accomplish.[27] As such, we found that having characteristics like a description of agencies' activities, roles, and responsibilities as part of a strategy helps to enhance the strategy's effectiveness. Strategies that include characteristics such as these provide policymakers and implementing agencies with a planning tool that can better help ensure accountability and more effective results.[28]

In addition to defining activities, roles, and responsibilities of participating agencies, the Strategy also defines its scope and purpose and identifies the problems, risks, and threats associated with transnational gangs. In our prior work, we found that desirable characteristics of effective national strategies also include a discussion of purpose, scope, problems, risks, and threats. For example, in defining its purpose and scope, the Strategy notes that effectively addressing the problem of these transnational gangs requires close coordination and information sharing among the affected countries in Central America and Mexico and a comprehensive approach that includes law enforcement, prevention, intervention, rehabilitation, and reintegration for gang members, which the five categories of the Strategy are intended to address. In regards to identifying the problem, the Strategy states that gangs such as MS-13 and 18th Street threaten U.S. regional interests in fostering stable democracies and the U.S. domestic interest in protecting U.S. citizens from gang violence and crime. These characteristics help indicate why the Strategy was developed and identify the specific national issues and threats toward which the Strategy is directed.

The Strategy's Lack of an Oversight Framework Hinders Efforts to Enhance Accountability

Even as the Strategy contains several characteristics of effective national strategies, it lacks other characteristics, such as providing an approach for overseeing implementation of programs and efforts across its different categories. Our prior work on effective national strategies found that they include an approach or framework for overseeing their implementation or describe the organizations that will provide oversight, which enhances the accountability of agencies and stakeholders to implement programs as planned.[29] This is especially important for the U.S. antigang strategy given that (1) there are eight federal departments or agencies involved in implementing the Strategy; (2) these agencies have wide-ranging missions and programs—from USAID's mission to implement gang prevention and youth intervention programs to ICE's mission to remove foreign-born gang members from the United States; and (3) the Strategy specifies 35 different activities under the five categories that federal agencies are to implement.

With regard to oversight, the Strategy itself does not identify an approach or framework for providing oversight across agencies' implementation of the Strategy's categories and activities and, according to DOJ, State, and USAID officials, one does not exist. Although the Strategy designates lead departments or agencies for each category, such as State leading the Diplomacy category and USAID leading the Prevention category, the Strategy does not designate an approach to provide oversight of the overall implementation of the Strategy across the Strategy's various categories. Further, while members of an interagency antigang task force have discussed agencies' efforts to implement the Strategy, this task force is not intended to provide this oversight. According to DOJ, State, and USAID officials, under the auspices of the NSC, the International Anti- Gang Task Force, which is chaired by DOJ's Criminal Division and includes representatives from DOJ, DHS, State, and USAID, has responsibility for sharing information on the implementation of the Strategy. However, this task force is not intended to, nor does it, provide oversight for holding agencies accountable for implementation of their activities under the Strategy. Additionally, State's regional gang advisor stated that no single department or entity has been identified as having oversight responsibility for the Strategy's implementation. DOJ officials did not know why an oversight mechanism was not included in the Strategy, noting that, as a result, there is no enforcement mechanism to ensure that agencies are implementing their respective parts of the Strategy. USAID officials told us that after the Strategy was developed, the individual within the NSC who had been responsible for coordinating development of the Strategy stated that the council's IOCPCC was to oversee the implementation of the Strategy; however this did not occur in part because the individual left the council. Additionally, although federal agencies are developing a strategy for the newly formed CARSI, participating agencies have not yet determined the oversight framework, if any, that is to be used for this broader initiative or whether the existing antigang Strategy will be incorporated into CARSI. Thus, it is too early to tell whether CARSI will provide an oversight approach for federal agencies' antigang programs. Regardless of whether the antigang Strategy is incorporated into the new CARSI, or whether the NSC or some other agency or entity is responsible for oversight, establishing an approach or framework for oversight across the Strategy's categories could help enhance the accountability of agencies to implement activities as laid out in the Strategy and provide visibility over the extent to which agencies' individual efforts are achieving their intended results under the Strategy.

The Strategy's Lack of Performance Goals and Measures Hinders Efforts to Assess Progress

Our prior work found that effective national strategies set clear goals and related performance measures for assessing progress made in achieving intended results. The Strategy, however, does not identify the goals that are to be achieved through its implementation and the associated measures to track the progress made in achieving those goals, which could be established and monitored through an oversight approach or framework. We have reported that performance measurement is important because decision makers can use performance information to identify problems or weaknesses in programs, identify factors causing problems, and modify processes to address the problems.[30] USAID officials told us that after the Strategy was initially developed, the NSC intended to establish performance measures for implementation of the Strategy, but this did not occur in part because the individual within the NSC who had been responsible for coordinating development of the Strategy left the council. Although the Strategy itself lacks goals and measures to gauge results and assess progress across the Strategy's categories and activities, State and USAID, for their parts of the Strategy, have begun to develop mechanisms to assess the results of their efforts being implemented under the Mérida Initiative, including the initiative's antigang programs. For example, for its part, State has drafted four gang-specific performance measures within the broader set of measures it is developing for the Mérida Initiative: (1) number of arrests of suspected gang members completed by police units trained/equipped through Mérida Initiative funding in countergang strategies, (2) number of arrests and prosecutions of gang leaders in the region, (3) number of gang-related crime occurrences and homicides in the region, and (4) number of instances where gang-related information is passed from the TAG to U.S. law enforcement for review/action. State officials noted that the department is working with its embassies to determine if Central American countries will be capable of providing the department with the requisite data needed to determine results and outcomes for these measures, as these countries control much of the data, often in disparate data sets and across various ministries. As of November 2009, State officials also reported that they were in the process of reviewing bids from contractors to develop performance measures for the department's Mérida Initiative programs, including its antigang programs, and to work directly with the host nations to obtain the necessary data to determine the results and outcomes of the efforts based on these measures.[31]

In addition to the measures State is developing to evaluate the results of Mérida Initiative-funded programs in Central America, USAID has developed a Mérida Initiative Central America Results Framework that includes an effect evaluation to be conducted by Vanderbilt University through a contractual arrangement with USAID. The agency intends for this evaluation to assess the long-term effect and measure the results of its programs in Central American communities that are the focus of USAID crime prevention efforts under the Mérida Initiative, including those related to gangs. The evaluation consists of five elements: (1) community surveys, (2) reviews of demographic data in the communities, (3) focus groups, (4) interviews with stakeholders such as community leaders, and (5) community observations such as physical infrastructure. Vanderbilt University officials are to conduct the evaluations every 18 months in communities where USAID-sponsored crime prevention activities have been implemented and communities where no activities have been implemented, with these latter communities serving as control groups in order to establish a baseline. Specifically with respect to the surveys, USAID plans to use the results to gauge the effect of its crime prevention programs through community and citizen perceptions on safety and security. To minimize any duplication and take advantage of survey efforts already underway, USAID officials stated that they plan to incorporate the survey questions on community and citizen perceptions on safety and security as part of a broader survey Vanderbilt University will be conducting in the region in 2010.

Although State and USAID have begun to develop mechanisms to help assess the outcomes of antigang programs implemented under the Mérida Initiative, these mechanisms do not encompass all of the Strategy's categories and activities, nor do they include the antigang programs of other federal agencies, such as those of DOJ and DHS. For example, while the measures State is developing, such as the numbers of arrests of gang members and leaders in the region, relate to the law enforcement, capacity enhancement, and prevention categories of the Strategy, these measures do not encompass the diplomacy or repatriation categories of the Strategy. According to State and USAID officials as well as officials from the FBI and ICE, State and USAID have not consulted or worked with DOJ and DHS agencies such as FBI and ICE in developing these performance measures because State's and USAID's measures are intended to encompass only their own programs and efforts. According to State, USAID, DOJ, and DHS officials, each agency focuses on developing performance-related goals and measures for its own programs as opposed to other agencies' antigang programs for which it is not responsible, and, therefore, less familiar. As a result, the performance measures State and USAID are developing cannot serve as overall indicators of the federal government's progress in implementing the Strategy as they do not take into account all of the federal agencies' antigang programs to be implemented under the Strategy's five categories, including those programs led by DOJ and DHS. In the absence of goals and performance measures or other mechanisms for monitoring and assessing the progress and performance of agencies' antigang programs across the categories of the Strategy, it will be difficult for the federal government to determine if the overall interagency antigang effort is achieving the intended results and to hold agencies accountable for implementing the Strategy.

U.S. Federal Agencies Have Implemented Programs to Combat Transnational Gangs, but Could Take Additional Action to Enhance Coordination Efforts

Federal agencies have implemented a variety of programs to carry out the Strategy and combat transnational gangs with connections to Central America. To coordinate their implementation of antigang programs, agencies use a variety of mechanisms such as interagency committees and task forces. However, for the antigang unit in El Salvador, coordination among the FBI, ICE, and Salvadoran law enforcement in sharing investigative information on gangs could be enhanced by reaching agreement on ICE's participation in the unit. Further, although agencies have taken steps to develop performance measures and obtain data on those measures to track the results of programs, agencies are just starting to collect performance data due to the early stage of implementation of most of these programs. Additionally, federal agencies have identified various factors that are largely outside their control and that can affect their implementation of programs, such as challenges facing Central American countries in sustaining antigang programs.

Federal Agencies Have Developed a Variety of Programs to Implement the Interagency Strategy

To carry out the Strategy and combat transnational gangs with connections to Central American countries, federal agencies have developed and implemented a variety of programs in the United States and in host countries in the region, such as El Salvador and Guatemala. This variety of programs reflects the different categories of the strategy and includes diplomatic efforts to establish a coordinated approach to the gang problem; efforts to facilitate the repatriation of gang members who are in the United States illegally; mechanisms to facilitate the sharing of investigative information between U.S. law enforcement agencies and foreign law enforcement agencies; programs to provide training to Central American law enforcement officials; and programs to provide recreational and vocational opportunities for at-risk youth, among others. Additional details on federal agencies' antigang programs under each category of the Strategy are as follows:[32]

- Diplomacy: State has led efforts to engage diplomatically with Central American countries to discuss gang issues. The department has led discussions with member countries of the Central American Integration System. Under this initiative, the United States and Central American countries first held discussions regarding regional gang threats in July 2007, at which time the United States announced the Strategy. The countries held a second, and the most recent, dialogue in December 2008, which focused on discussing practical measures to combat the threats of criminal gangs, narcotics trafficking, and illicit trafficking of firearms in Central

America. At the conclusion, all participating countries signed a communiqué pledging their continued support in the fight against transnational threats, including gangs.

- Repatriation: ICE has implemented the Electronic Travel Document system to facilitate the issuance of travel documents for the removal of illegal aliens, including gang members, to El Salvador, Guatemala, and Honduras. Under this program, ICE electronically sends travel document applications to the consular officials of these countries; these officials can then electronically sign and certify the documents stating that the countries will receive the illegal aliens to be removed.[33] These documents are available to ICE electronically through the Electronic Travel Document system. This program eliminates the need for consular officials to visit in person the individual awaiting removal from the United States before issuing documents, helping to reduce the amount of time it takes for ICE to receive travel documents from foreign countries and ultimately remove illegal aliens. According to ICE officials, the program can eliminate approximately 5 to 7 days that an alien would spend in detention, thus decreasing the cost incurred by the government.
- Law Enforcement: In 2005, ICE implemented Operation Community Shield—a nationwide initiative to arrest and remove criminal alien gang members from the United States. ICE began the operation to target violent transnational street gangs through the use of ICE's broad law enforcement powers to identify, prosecute, and ultimately remove gang members from the United States. Although initially focused on MS-13, ICE expanded Operation Community Shield to target all transnational criminal street gangs, prison gangs, and outlaw motorcycle gangs. For its part, the FBI has implemented various programs to facilitate the exchange of information, such as criminal histories of suspected gang members, between law enforcement agencies in the United States and Central American countries. For example, in 2007, the FBI established a joint U.S.- Salvadoran Transnational Anti-Gang unit in El Salvador—called TAG—to exchange information on gangs and gang members between the Salvadoran national police and U.S.-based law enforcement agencies for use in criminal investigations and gang-member prosecutions in both countries. The unit includes investigators and analysts from the Salvadoran national police, prosecutors from El Salvador's Attorney General's Office, and two FBI agents. The TAG unit's exchange of information on gang members has aided U.S. gang investigations in locations such as Charlotte, North Carolina; Omaha, Nebraska; and Los Angeles, California. The FBI plans to establish units like this in Guatemala and Honduras. Further, in 2006, the FBI began the Central American Fingerprint Exploitation program to collect and store existing criminal fingerprint records and other biometric information from the countries of Mexico, El Salvador, Guatemala, Belize, and Honduras in FBI databases and make them available to all U.S. local, state, and federal law enforcement agencies. These records are searched in the FBI's Integrated Automated Fingerprint Identification System, with resulting matches shared with the contributing country for investigative purposes.[34] The FBI has deployed the system in El Salvador, conducted assessments to determine how to deploy the system to Belize and Panama, and plans to conduct more assessments for deploying the system to Guatemala and Honduras. In addition, beginning in 2008, the FBI, with funding from State, has implemented the Central American Law

Enforcement Exchange program wherein law enforcement personnel from El Salvador, Guatemala, and Honduras have visited locations in the United States to receive antigang training and share investigative practices with U.S. law enforcement personnel. In exchange, law enforcement personnel from the United States have visited El Salvador to provide antigang training and share practices with Central American police.[35] Also related to law enforcement, ICE, in conjunction with State, established an international gang task force in Honduras in January 2010. Comprised of four Honduran police officers and one ICE agent, the task force is charged with developing intelligence to initiate and support gang investigations in the United States and Honduras.

- Capacity Enhancement: To help enhance the capacity of Central American governments to address gangs, beginning in 2006, State, DOJ, DHS, and other agencies have provided antigang training courses to Central American law enforcement officials through the International Law Enforcement Academy in El Salvador.[36] The academy provides law enforcement training to officials from countries in Central and South America and the Caribbean. The training courses have focused on various aspects of gang enforcement efforts, such as police investigative techniques, prosecution, witness protection, and prison gang management, and participants have included police, prosecutors, judges, prison staff, border agents, and prevention and rehabilitation officials from El Salvador, Guatemala, Honduras, Mexico, Panama, and Belize. As another example of capacity enhancement, USAID has provided technical assistance and training to police, prosecutors, and judges, among others, to reform justice-sector institutions in El Salvador to help improve the investigation, prosecution, and prevention of crimes including those committed by gangs.
- Prevention: USAID has implemented gang prevention, intervention, and rehabilitation programs in Central American countries to provide youth with alternatives to joining gangs and assist former gang members' reentry into society. For example, through partnerships with faith-based and nongovernmental organizations and local governments in Central America, USAID has started youth centers in specific communities to provide a safe environment for recreational and vocational opportunities for young people. Figure 2 shows individuals participating in activities at these youth centers in El Salvador.

Additionally, USAID has sponsored a community-based policing program in Guatemala to improve the relationship between the police and local citizens by establishing collaborative partnerships between law enforcement and the communities they serve to solve problems and increase trust. According to USAID, the agency plans to expand the community policing program to five new communities in Guatemala as well as five communities each in El Salvador and Panama.

Source: GAO.
Youth participating in a computer repair class (left) and a baking class (right).
Note: The photographs have been altered to protect identities.

Figure 2. Youth Participating in Activities at USAID-sponsored Youth Centers in El Salvador

Federal Agencies Have Coordinated Their Antigang Programs through Various Mechanisms, but Could Strengthen Coordination by Examining the Establishment and Composition of a Salvadoran-Based Law Enforcement Unit

Federal agencies have taken action to coordinate their antigang programs and share information with each other through various interagency and coordinating groups. For example, DOJ has established several entities to coordinate and share information on gang enforcement efforts, including transnational gangs, among DOJ and DHS component agencies. These entities include the Anti-Gang Coordination Committee that is comprised of representatives from a variety of DOJ components and agencies, as well as representatives from DHS's ICE, and meets at least quarterly each year to report on the status of antigang efforts and disseminate information for coordination. Another entity used to coordinate, share information and intelligence on gangs, and serve as a deconfliction center for gang operations is the National Gang Targeting, Enforcement, and Coordination Center (GangTECC).[37] GangTECC is comprised of participants from the FBI, ATF, DEA, and ICE, among other DOJ and DHS components, and has responsibility for coordinating multijurisdictional investigations of all gangs except FBI-led investigations involving the MS-13 and 18th Street gangs. In addition, the FBI's MS-13 National Gang Task Force has only FBI participants and is responsible for coordinating FBI's multijurisdictional investigations involving MS-13 and 18th Street gangs. Further, within Central American countries, federal agencies have mechanisms for coordinating and sharing information on antigang programs. For example, in El Salvador at the U.S. embassy, U.S. government agency officials who are involved in implementing antigang programs, such as officials from DOJ, DHS, State, USAID, and DOD, hold regular meetings to discuss antigang activities and coordinate their implementation efforts. Appendix IV provides additional information on the roles and responsibilities of these and other headquarters-level coordinating entities as well as task forces that coordinate antigang efforts at the field level within the United States.

In July 2009, we reported on the benefits and challenges associated with some of these various coordinating mechanisms. Specifically, we reported that entities such as the Anti-Gang Coordination Committee, GangTECC, and the MS-13 National Gang Task Force provide DOJ and DHS with a means to operate across agency boundaries and facilitate communication among participating agencies at the headquarters level.[38] However, we also reported that while some overlaps in mission may be appropriate, the entities had not clearly identified their roles and responsibilities, resulting in possible gaps or unnecessary overlaps in agencies' coordination and sharing of information on gang enforcement efforts, including those involving transnational gangs. Specifically, we reported that GangTECC and the MS-13 National Gang Task Force had overlapping missions and responsibilities for coordination and deconfliction of multijurisdictional investigations involving the MS-13 and 18th Street gangs. The two entities had these overlaps in part because the MS-13 National Gang Task Force already existed when GangTECC was established in 2006 and was not dismantled or folded into GangTECC at that time. We reported that both entities risked unnecessary federal resource expenditures to fund two entities when a single group could be more efficient. We recommended that DOJ, in consultation with DHS, articulate and differentiate roles, responsibilities, and missions of headquarters-level entities, which would strengthen headquarters-level coordination efforts to help ensure that they are not expended on overlapping missions. DOJ agreed with our recommendation and as of February 2010, DHS and DOJ officials reported that they are discussing ways to streamline processes, modify policies, and establish cross-cutting performance measures for federal gang programs.

At the field level, FBI and ICE could strengthen their coordination and sharing of information on gang members and investigations specifically in El Salvador by reaching agreement on ICE's participation in the TAG.[39] In El Salvador, both ICE and FBI contact the Salvadoran national police to request information and intelligence on gangs to assist in the agencies' gang investigations. The FBI makes its requests directly through its agents assigned to the TAG, while ICE's requests for Salvadoran national police information on gangs or gang members are sent through ICE's country attaché in El Salvador who forwards them to the FBI agents at the TAG. The FBI agents then pass the requests to Salvadoran national police officials if the FBI agents do not have the information needed to fulfill ICE's requests.[40] FBI and ICE officials stated that this process for coordinating information requests for the Salvadoran national police through the TAG has worked well, but that the process could be further strengthened by ICE's participation in the TAG unit. Our work on effective interagency coordination has shown that collaborating agencies should organize joint and individual efforts and facilitate information sharing.[41] Collaborating agencies also look for opportunities to leverage each others' resources, thus obtaining additional benefits that would not be available if they were working separately. Coordinating in this way could yield benefits in terms of leveraging efforts already underway and minimizing any potential unnecessary duplication in federal agencies' requests for information on gang members or gang investigations. Various U.S. and Salvadoran officials have cited potential benefits that could be gained from ICE and FBI both participating in the TAG. The director of El Salvador's national police stated that he would like to see federal law enforcement agencies other than the FBI involved in the TAG unit, particularly ICE, because of ICE's role in managing the removal of gang members from the United States to El Salvador. The unit chief of FBI's MS-13 National Gang Task Force stated that the FBI would also benefit from ICE participating in the TAG to assist in deconflicting enforcement operations between the FBI and ICE in El Salvador. ICE's El Salvador country attaché stated that having an ICE agent at the TAG would streamline the current process since an ICE agent would be working directly at the TAG and be able to better identify possible connections between FBI and ICE gang cases and requests for information, thereby expediting information sharing.

The FBI and ICE have discussed signing a joint memorandum of understanding to provide parameters for ICE's participation in the TAG. According to the unit chief of the FBI's MS-13 National Gang Task Force, in 2008 the FBI presented ICE with a memorandum of understanding for ICE to participate in the TAG unit in which the FBI legal attaché would manage the TAG and coordinate TAG gang investigations with ICE. The FBI memorandum required ICE to coordinate all of its activities related to the TAG with the FBI legal attaché. However, according to the head of ICE's National Gang Unit, ICE would like to participate in the TAG more as an equal partner as opposed to being subordinate to the FBI. ICE officials stated that clarification is needed in regards to the administrative details on placing an ICE agent at the TAG such as housing and the location of the ICE agent's office, as well as agreement on the extent to which an ICE agent assigned to the TAG could focus on work for ICE- specific investigations as needed.

To help obtain this clarification and try to reach consensus on ICE participation in TAG, ICE officials stated that as of February 2010 they have not yet completed the process of drafting language to clarify their points of concern in the memorandum of understanding and plan to provide this draft language, once completed, to the FBI for its consideration. Further, the FBI and ICE have initiated discussions to conduct an assessment of ICE's possible participation in TAG by having an ICE agent who would conduct the assessment assigned to the unit on a temporary basis. However, as of February 2010, ICE and FBI have not yet reached agreement on this temporary assignment and ICE's plans to conduct the assessment because the two agencies disagree about the type and scope of the work that the agent would conduct for the assessment. The FBI and ICE could strengthen their coordination on gang investigations and enhance the efficiency of their existing process for exchanging information through the TAG by reaching consensus on ICE's participation in the unit. By reaching agreement on ICE's role, which the FBI and ICE have been considering since 2008, the two agencies would be in a better position to leverage their existing resources and information-sharing processes for gang investigations with a nexus to El Salvador.

Federal Agencies Have Established Performance Measures for Their Own Antigang Programs, but Some Programs Are in the Early Stages of Collecting Performance Data

Earlier in this chapter, we discussed federal government efforts to measure the results achieved with the overall Strategy. Separately, federal agencies have established performance measures, such as numbers of arrests of gang members, for assessing their own individual antigang efforts. However, as most of these programs are in the early stages of implementation, agencies' data on their programs' performance cannot yet be used to assess the level of activity or program results across time. For example, USAID officials said that because most of the Mérida Initiative funding for its Central American programs was not released to USAID field missions until July and August 2009, programs funded by the Mérida

Initiative have yet to have any appreciable results to measure. In addition, several antigang programs in Central America have yet to be fully implemented. For example, ICE and the FBI are seeking to establish the Criminal History Information Program in El Salvador, Guatemala, and Honduras pending the hiring of needed analysts and completion of interagency agreements—expected to occur by the summer of 2010.

Although federal agencies' performance data do not yet indicate the level of progress or results achieved over time, federal agencies have begun to report data on their levels of activity to date. For example, State has established measures for the antigang training courses offered through the International Law Enforcement Academy in El Salvador, including tracking data on the number of gang classes offered and the number of participants successfully completing them. According to State, the academy has offered 10 gang-related training courses since 2006 with a total of 416 participants from various countries including El Salvador, Honduras, Guatemala, and Mexico. In addition to these measures, State asks participants to complete course evaluations and uses these evaluations to make modifications to the antigang training courses, such as changes in curriculum.

USAID has also established measures for its own antigang programs, as shown in table 2. For example, USAID has established measures for its community policing program, such as the number of communities that have implemented community policing programs.

Table 2. Examples of Measures USAID Tracks for Its Efforts to Combat Transnational Gangs from Central America

Activity/ program	Description of program	Date began	Examples of measures to be tracked
Community Action Fund	Provide employment-generating activities and education for youth at risk of gang involvement	2008	Number of people who have benefited from U.S. government-supported educational and socioeconomic opportunities
Community Policing Program	Promotes collaboration between communities and police in pre-vention activities to undermine gang effectiveness and recruit-ment, resulting in successful arrests of gang members and greatly improved cooperation and trust between the police and citizens of the communities	2008	Number of communities with joint police-citizen groups (e.g., community committees, police/ school liaison, police/citizen activities, etc.)
Gang Prevention Program	Increases security through com-munity and private-sector par-tnerships that work with at-risk youth to reduce gang recruitm-ent, crime, and violence by building the capacity of comm.-unities and governments and by enhancing law enforcement efforts	2008	Number of communities assisted in crime prevention with U.S. government support

Source: GAO analysis of USAID data.

Note: Data sources include conversations with agency officials.

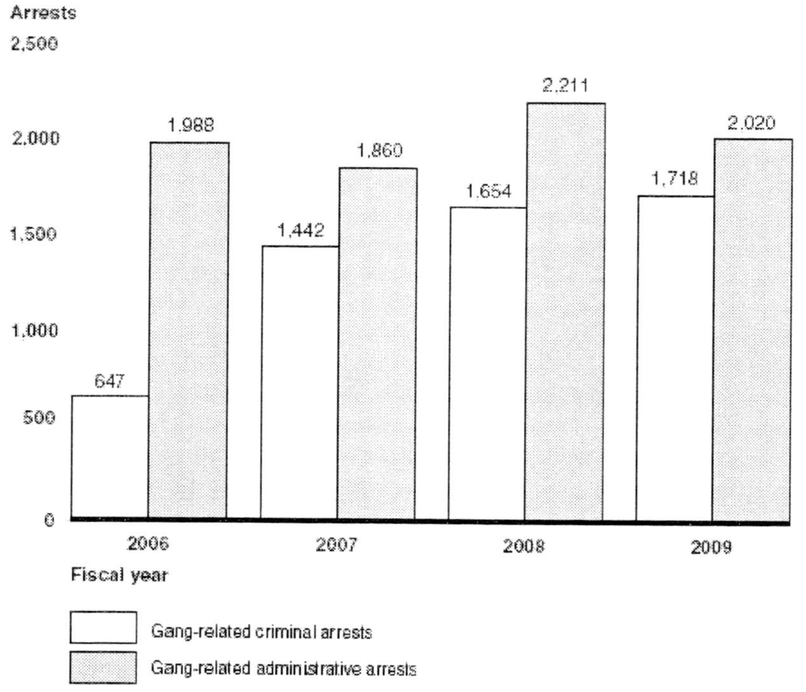

Source: ICE.

Figure 3. ICE Gang-Related Arrests (Fiscal Years 2006 through 2009)

USAID also requires program contractors to develop performance indexes for their respective programs. For example, the private contractor conducting USAID's Community-based Crime and Violence Prevention Project plans to review local government records to measure the crime rate in project-targeted communities. For other efforts related to youth outreach centers, performance indicators tracked by program contractors include measures such as the number of youth who have received a job through the support of the outreach center or because of the skills acquired through the center.

With regard to its gang enforcement efforts, ICE reports on the number of gang-related criminal and administrative arrests, among other measures.[42] As shown in figure 3, the number of criminal and administrative gang- related arrests made by ICE has generally increased since fiscal year 2006, the first full year that it compiled this information.

As shown in table 3, the FBI has also established various measures for each of its primary programs to combat transnational gangs. Among others, these measures include the number of gang cases worked and the number of countries and officials participating in the Central American Law Enforcement Exchange Program.

In addition to these measures, the FBI has prepared after-action reports for the Central American Law Enforcement Exchange Program that summarize the results of the exchanges, including feedback from program participants, and has used these reports to modify the program. For example, according to the FBI, future exchange classes will include more practical and operational experiences (such as ride-alongs with local police officers and observation of police operations). Moreover, future classes will include more allowances for travel time and representation from more U.S. and foreign police departments.

Table 3. Performance Measures and Reported Results for the FBI's Efforts to Combat Transnational Gangs

FBI program/ activity	Performance measure	Outputs reported
MS-13 National Gang Task Force	• Number of gang cases worked. • Number of coordination meetings with FBI Field Divisions and legal attaches. • Training provided to federal, state, local, and international law enforcement partners.	• According to the FBI, the task force conducted 19 investigations in fiscal year 2007, 29 investigations in fiscal year 2008, and 140 investigations in fiscal year 2009. • The task force reported conducting 10 case-coordination meetings in fiscal year 2007, 15 meetings in fiscal year 2008, and 23 meetings in fiscal year 2009. • The task force reported conducting 12 trainings for law enforcement partners in fiscal year 2007, 10 trainings in fiscal year 2008, and 15 trainings in fiscal year 2009.
TAG unit	Number of requests for information received by the TAG to investigate leads on suspected gang members including whether a "hit" was made on the lead (i.e., a positive result).	During fiscal year 2008, the first year the FBI tracked perform-ance metrics for the TAG, coun-tries including El Salvador made 696 inquiries regarding transn-ational connections of suspected gang members. For fiscal year 2009, the FBI reported a total of 480 inquiries to the TAG.
	Number of contraband items recovered during TAG-assisted prison searches in El Salvador.	The FBI reported that 27 prison searches were conducted between September 2007 and November 2009. Over 1,000 items were seized during these prison searches.
	The number of arrests made by El Salvadoran law enforcement working in antigang operations who received coaching, advice, and instruction from the TAG unit	According to the FBI, from the TAG's inception in September 2007 to July 2009, 16 gang members were arrested.
Central American Law Enforcement Exchange Program	Number of countries and officials participating in the program.	FBI officials reported that in 2008, four officers from El Salv-ador and four officers from the United States (Los Angeles) part-icipated in the first version of this program, which was referred to as the "Officer Exchange Program."
		According to the FBI's after-action report, "Exchange Class I" was conducted in March 2009 consisting of 27 participants representing four countries and nine law enforcement

Table 3. (Continued)

FBI program/ activity	Performance measure	Outputs reported
		organizat-ions. In addition to the United States, the countries included El Salvador, Honduras, and Guate-mala. In October 2009, 27 offi-cers from law enforcement agencies in the United States, El Salvador, Guatemala, Nicaragua, and Panama participated in a third exchange.
Central American Fingerprint Exploitation	Number of positive hits from foreign fingerprint data for subjects with U.S. criminal histories. The MS-13 National Gang Task Force maintains a record of all positive hits, warrants, and sexual offenders who are located.	According to FBI officials, app-roximately 3 million criminal fin-gerprint records from Central America and Mexico have been acquired. In particular, El Salv-ador, the only Central American country where the FBI has fully implemented the Central Amer-ican Fingerprint Exploitation, has provided 75,000 fingerprint records in fiscal year 2009 to the FBI with 10,556 matches against U.S. criminal records for a match rate of approximately 15 percent.

Source: GAO analysis of FBI data.

For the TAG, the FBI did not start to collect data for the unit's measures, such as the number of requests for assistance the unit receives, until April 2008, about 6 months after the unit was established. According to FBI officials, no systematic log or other mechanism was used to track and record data on the TAG's activities from September 2007 through April 2008, because, at the start-up of the unit, agents were assigned on a temporary basis and were primarily focused on establishing and initiating the operations of the unit. Thus, the FBI lacks information about the unit's activity levels for its first 6 months of operation. Since FBI agents have been stationed at the TAG for 2-year, long-term rotations, these agents have developed and maintained a log to track the unit's activities and assistance provided to FBI offices and other law enforcement agencies. This data maintained by the TAG is used by FBI, particularly the MS-13 National Gang Task Force, to identify trends in where transnational gang members are located and traveling to and proactively target specific geographic areas for gang education or enforcement activities.

Various Factors Affect U.S. Efforts to Implement Antigang Programs in Central American Countries

Even as agencies have worked to implement antigang programs in Central America, various factors in the region largely outside of the control of U.S. agencies pose challenges to the implementation of the programs. These factors include: the ability of host countries to sustain programs after U.S. support ends; Central American law enforcement personnel issues; and legal restrictions in Central American countries, such as El Salvador, that diminish the benefits of efforts.

- Sustainability of programs by host countries: Federal agencies have identified challenges facing Central American countries in sustaining antigang programs currently being initiated and implemented in the region. Specifically, State officials identified several factors outside the control of U.S. agencies that contribute to the uncertainty as to whether Central American countries will be able to sustain antigang programs over the long term. These officials reported that the ability of partner countries to take responsibility for managing and supporting U.S.-funded antigang programs is hampered by the fact that these countries often do not have the financial resources to sustain the programs in the absence of U.S. funds. State officials said that the ability of foreign countries to sustain antigang programs is hindered by other factors as well, such as corruption throughout the countries' police and judiciary structures; a lack of investment in police training to make the countries' police forces more professional and accountable; the countries' inability to provide police forces with equipment such as communications gear and transportation assets; and the ability of the gangs to quickly adapt to law enforcement strategies.
- To help address these issues, federal agencies have taken steps prior to implementing these programs to plan for how the programs will be sustained, particularly after U.S. federal funding ends. For example, State officials said that when the department first developed and implemented these programs, it took into account the ability of foreign countries to take over and manage antigang programs initially funded and managed by the United States. Specifically, the officials noted that they worked directly with host country officials to gain an understanding of what programs or efforts the countries needed and what the countries might be able to support, both in terms of resources available and a supportive political climate, and then used that as a starting point to identify and shape the efforts that would receive U.S. support. According to USAID officials, USAID also took similar steps to work with host country officials to identify antigang efforts the countries had planned or were already underway for which USAID could provide additional support. Officials stated that they chose this approach because they sought to support local initiatives and programs whenever possible, as programs already planned or implemented by the host countries are more likely to be sustained by the countries themselves. Rather than setting up similar programs that would compete for resources, providing support for the host countries' programs helped to broaden the reach of the programs into additional areas that the host countries may not have had resources for otherwise. Further, USAID officials reported that they coordinated with the host countries and other donors to ensure that the host countries would assume responsibility for the activities when USAID funding expires. In regard to FBI-led efforts such as the TAG, FBI officials stated that they also considered the ability of the foreign government to support these efforts during negotiations between the foreign governments, such as El Salvador, and the FBI to establish the units.
- To help prepare for sustaining antigang programs over the long term, federal agencies have also taken action after these programs have been implemented. For example, at the country level, USAID officials work directly with host government

partners and with other donors through regular donor coordination groups and meetings to identify best practices for sustaining efforts and incorporating those practices into programs. Further, FBI officials have discussed with the Salvadoran government ways for the government to provide the resources and commitment needed to help sustain the TAG unit over the long term. According to the unit chief of the MS-13 National Gang Task Force who manages the TAG, other than what the FBI pays for in the salaries and living expenses of the FBI agents based at the TAG, the Salvadoran government provides the other resources necessary to sustain the TAG's operations.

- Screening process for law enforcement personnel and transfer of personnel: Finding a sufficient number of Central American law enforcement personnel who can pass the screening process required to participate in U.S. investigative and information-sharing programs can complicate the implementation of those programs. For example, in order to become part of the FBI's TAG unit, police officers must receive a background screening before initially joining the unit and undergo a polygraph every 6 months thereafter. Under the rules of the TAG, if officers fail the polygraph, they must leave the unit. FBI officials stated that, as was the case in El Salvador when they set up the TAG in that country, they expect to face challenges in identifying and successfully screening a sufficient number of Guatemalan and Honduran police officers to participate in the units planned for those countries.[43] To address this challenge, the FBI is planning to establish smaller TAG units in Guatemala and Honduras (10 officers each instead of the 20 stationed at the Salvadoran TAG) and set aside more time and resources for screening Guatemalan and Honduran police officers for the units. FBI officials also stated that one disadvantage of the first officer exchange with El Salvador was that of the four participating Salvadoran police officers, only two officers continued to work on gang investigations in El Salvador after the exchange was completed with the other two being transferred to different areas within the Salvadoran police force. Although the FBI has an agreement with participating countries that requires exchange participants to be involved in gang investigations for at least 2 years after the exchange has concluded so they can put into practice the training they received and share it with their colleagues, FBI officials noted that there is little they can do to ensure participating countries abide by this requirement.
- Legal restrictions: According to officials we interviewed from the FBI and DOJ's Criminal Division, Central American countries' laws can also pose challenges for conducting gang investigations in the region, or for federal agencies that may seek the extradition of individuals to face trial for crimes committed in the United States. According to an FBI official with the MS-13 National Gang Task Force, legal restrictions in countries such as El Salvador do not permit law enforcement to conduct electronic surveillance or wiretaps as part of their investigations. According to this official, while this restriction has not hindered the ability of the Salvadoran national police to conduct investigations, it takes more time and effort to develop and corroborate the evidence through the use of other investigative methods. According to an official from DOJ's Criminal Division, a recent amendment to the Salvadoran constitution now allows the use of electronic surveillance as a tool in criminal investigations and the Salvadoran National Assembly is currently considering

implementing legislation. In regard to the extradition of gang members wanted in the United States, FBI officials noted that countries such as El Salvador have laws that prohibit the extradition of individuals to other countries where they could face a more severe punishment than would be given in El Salvador for the same crime. As an example, the unit chief of the MS-13 National Gang Task Force stated that the FBI had requested the extradition of a gang leader imprisoned in El Salvador for prosecution in Baltimore, Maryland, where the individual would have likely faced a longer prison sentence for the crime. However, the FBI's request for extradition was denied, preventing the gang leader from facing the charges against him in the United States. Nevertheless, DOJ's Criminal Division reported that on December 22, 2009, the Supreme Court of El Salvador voted to permit the first extradition of a Salvadoran national pursuant to the extradition treaty between the United States and El Salvador.[44] Officials explained that future extraditions may still be limited by the penalties applicable to extradited individuals, such as the death penalty and life imprisonment. To help address these challenges, DOJ's Criminal Division continues to work with El Salvador under the existing treaty to facilitate extradition between the United States and El Salvador.

- Despite these challenges, officials from the agencies we interviewed stated that they continue to work to address or mitigate the effect of these challenges and to ensure their antigang programs are both sustainable and effective.

CONCLUSIONS

Given the rapid growth of transnational gangs, their propensity for violence, and the public safety threats they pose, the response to these gangs requires a comprehensive and collaborative approach on the part of federal agencies that have different responsibilities and missions for combating transnational gangs. The Strategy to Combat the Threat of Criminal Gangs from Central America and Mexico (the Strategy) provides a roadmap for federal departments and agencies to follow in designing and implementing efforts to combat the gangs. However, while individual federal agencies may be familiar with the implementation of their own antigang programs, or those in the Strategy for which they are responsible, they do not necessarily have the visibility across the Strategy's categories to determine the extent to which the broader strategy is being implemented. Regardless as to whether it remains a separate effort or is incorporated into the broader CARSI being developed, incorporating an approach for overseeing the interagency effort to combat transnational gangs would help provide visibility by designating an agency or entity to ensure that the Strategy is being implemented as planned. In addition, as the Strategy and related antigang efforts are implemented, it will be important to be able to track the effect the Strategy as a whole is having against the transnational gang problem. By establishing performance goals and measures or other mechanisms to evaluate the progress made in implementing the Strategy, federal agencies, Congress, and other stakeholders could have more specific information relating to agencies' performance under the Strategy, thereby enabling them to make more informed decisions as to what adjustments to the Strategy might be necessary, if any, to achieve its desired effect. Relatedly, while federal agencies have taken various actions to collaborate on their transnational antigang efforts, agencies such as the FBI and ICE can take steps to further resolve their roles and participation in the TAG unit in El Salvador, especially given that the FBI and ICE have been discussing this participation since 2008. By reaching agreement on ICE's participation in the unit, both agencies could realize additional information-sharing benefits not only with each other, but with foreign counterparts, and help ensure that resources to combat gangs in El Salvador are used efficiently and effectively.

RECOMMENDATIONS FOR EXECUTIVE ACTION

To strengthen oversight and accountability for implementation of the Strategy to Combat the Threat of Criminal Gangs from Central America and Mexico (the Strategy), we recommend that the Special Assistant to the President for National Security Affairs, in conjunction with DOJ, DHS, State, USAID, and DOD, revise the Strategy to include, or include in the CARSI if the Strategy is incorporated into that initiative

- an approach or framework for overseeing implementation of the Strategy and antigang efforts in Central America, and
- performance goals and measures to assess progress made in achieving intended results under the Strategy.

To strengthen federal agencies' coordination of antigang efforts and maximize use of federal law enforcement resources in El Salvador, we recommend that the Attorney General and the Secretary of Homeland Security reach agreement on ICE's role and participation in the TAG unit.

AGENCY COMMENTS AND OUR EVALUATION

We provided a draft of this chapter for review to the Departments of Defense (DOD), Homeland Security (DHS), Justice (DOJ), and State (State); the U.S. Agency for International Development (USAID); and the National Security Council (NSC). DHS, DOJ, and USAID provided written comments on the draft report. DOD, State, and the NSC did not provide comments.

In their written comments, DHS and DOJ concurred with our recommendation that the Attorney General and the Secretary of Homeland Security reach agreement on ICE's role and participation in the TAG unit in El Salvador, and outlined steps they have begun to take to address this recommendation. For example, DHS commented that ICE officials have reviewed the FBI's memorandum on the TAG to clarify the roles and responsibilities of ICE and the FBI within the unit in El Salvador. DOJ also commented that any agreement on DHS's participation in the TAG unit in El Salvador should also address DHS's participation in future TAG units that the FBI expects to create in Guatemala and Honduras.

In its written comments, USAID commented that it acknowledges the importance of increased interagency coordination to help bolster U.S. government efforts to address the threat of criminal gangs in Central America and the United States.

DHS's, DOJ's, and USAID's written comments are contained in appendixes VI, VII, and VIII, respectively. We also incorporated technical comments provided by DHS, DOJ, and USAID as appropriate.

APPENDIX I. LEADERSHIP STRUCTURE AND KEY TRANSNATIONAL CRIMINAL ACTIVITIES OF MS-13 AND 18TH STREET

Federal agencies have specifically identified two primary gangs with connections to Central America—Mara Salvatrucha (MS-13) and 18th Street—as posing the most significant public safety threats to the United States and Central American countries among transnational gangs. This appendix summarizes information federal agencies have on the leadership structure and transnational criminal activities of these two gangs.

Leadership of the Gangs

Federal agencies have reported that these gangs generally do not have a centralized leadership structure. Rather, most gang cliques—or local gang groups—tend to operate in specific areas or communities in the United States and Central America and have autonomy to function independently without reporting to a central authority or leadership. However, law enforcement officials have reported that in some gang cliques activities are directed by gang leaders incarcerated in Salvadoran prisons. These leaders communicate by cell phones or coded written messages that are smuggled in and out of the prisons. Of the five U.S. locations[45] we visited to discuss gang investigations with federal, state, and local law enforcement, three reported instances in which gang leaders incarcerated in El Salvador directed gang members to organize new cliques, coordinate with cliques in other parts of the country, and carry out criminal activities, including murder. For example, an investigation in Charlotte, North Carolina, found that MS-13 clique leaders were sent to establish cliques at the behest of leaders in El Salvador. Further, according to the FBI, cliques convene periodically with gang leadership to determine future criminal activities and punishments for individual delinquent gang members.

Transnational Criminal Activities of the Gangs

Transnational gangs engage in criminal activities that not only affect local communities in the United States and Central American countries, but that also stretch beyond U.S. and Central American borders. For example, in its 2006 Central America and Mexico Gang Assessment, U.S. Agency for International Development (USAID) reported that gang activity has transcended the borders of Central America, Mexico, and the United States and evolved into a transnational concern.[46] USAID reported that while gang activity used to be territorially confined to local neighborhoods, globalization, sophisticated communications technologies, and travel patterns have facilitated the expansion of gang activity across neighborhoods, cities, and countries. Further, the 2009 National Gang Threat Assessment indicated that U.S.

street gangs are expanding their influence in most regions and broadening their presence outside the United States to develop associations with criminal organizations in Mexico and Central America. According to federal agencies, major cross- border criminal activities in which transnational gangs engage include drug trafficking and distribution, human smuggling, and extortion, among others.

With regard to drug trafficking and distribution, assessments conducted by the National Gang Intelligence Center, the National Drug Intelligence Center, the U.S. Agency for International Development, and the Federal Bureau of Investigation (FBI) indicate that connections exist between drug trafficking organizations and MS-13 and 18th Street gangs and these connections may be expanding. Several agencies also suggested that both gangs' connections with prison gangs such as the Mexican Mafia[47] may provide a link to drug trafficking organizations, as one of the prison gangs' main sources of income is extorting money from drug distributors outside prison and distributing various narcotics within and outside the prison system. Further, the U.S. Southern Command (SOUTHCOM) has reported that drug trafficking organizations have worked with MS-13 and 18th Street gangs to distribute their narcotics in Central America and the United States.[48] MS-13 and 18th Street gangs have also been identified as engaging in retail street distribution of narcotics in the United States, for example. Although connections between gangs and drug trafficking organizations exist and may be growing, these connections may not yet reflect large-scale, organized cooperation between gangs and drug- trafficking organizations. For example, Drug Enforcement Administration (DEA) officials stated that while individual gangs and gang members might work with drug trafficking organizations for their own personal gain, DEA has not observed or obtained evidence of high-level, organized cooperation between gangs and drug trafficking organizations. Likewise, the United Nations Office on Drugs and Crime has reported that because the Central American drug market is too small for gangs to develop into major distributors, the gangs lack the maritime capabilities required for the transport of drugs from Central America, and gangs have limited involvement in the U.S. narcotics market, the link between Central American gangs and drug trafficking organizations may not yet be well- developed.

In addition to their involvement in drug trafficking and distribution, transnational gangs have also been involved in other cross-border crime, including alien smuggling and extortion. For example, the 2009 National Gang Threat Assessment indicated that U.S.-based gang members are increasingly involved in cross-border criminal activity that includes smuggling illegal aliens from Mexico into the United States. Moreover, U.S. Customs and Border Protection and the FBI reported that MS-13 is known to smuggle persons from Central America into the United States from Mexico. The FBI has also reported that 18th Street may be involved in human trafficking and alien smuggling. However, the FBI stated that it is difficult to determine gang members' roles—whether they are organizing the border crossings, smuggling other aliens into the country, or being smuggled themselves.

In addition, federal agencies have reported that extortion and retail drug distribution provide financial support for both MS-13 and 18th Street. Cliques have been reported to extort those who conduct illicit activities themselves, such as prostitution or drug distribution entities, within the gangs' territory. In the United States, transnational gang members are known also to extort money from businesses that operate within gang territory in exchange for not inflicting harm on the businesses or those businesses' owners, family members, or workers. Both MS-13 and 18th Street gangs also conduct extortion across international borders. For example, gang members in the United States may extort immigrants with threats that they will retaliate against family members in Central America if law enforcement is notified. In some instances, the gangs have coupled extortion with kidnapping. The FBI has reported that MS-13 has kidnapped illegal immigrants and then extorted money from their families for the immigrants' safe return.

Finally, with regard to links to terrorists, federal agencies have found no indication that U.S. gangs with transnational ties have routine relationships.

APPENDIX II. CHARACTERISTICS OF OTHER TRANSNATIONAL GANGS

According to the National Gang Intelligence Center (NGIC), three basic types of gangs have been identified by gang investigators: street gangs, prison gangs, and outlaw motorcycle gangs. The focus of this chapter has been on gangs with ties to Central America, such as Mara Salvatrucha (MS- 13) and 18th Street, which belong to the "street gang" category. However, all three categories contain gangs with members who are either present or criminally active (or both) in more than one country. This appendix provides examples of other gangs in these categories, including descriptions of their transnational activities. Most of the information presented in this appendix is from the April 2008 Attorney General's Report to Congress on the Growth of Violent Street Gangs in Suburban Areas and supplemented by information obtained from interviews with agency officials.

Street Gangs

According to federal law enforcement, street gangs are typically associated with a particular neighborhood, town, or city, which they may incorporate into the name of their gang. However, law enforcement officials report that several street gangs have attained regional or national status and operate in a number of states throughout the country. Two examples of these street gangs that also have transnational connections include the following:

- Florencia 13: Florencia 13 originated in Los Angeles in the early 1960s. Gang membership is estimated to be more than 3,000. This gang operates primarily in California, but is expanding to other states. Drug trafficking is a primary source of income for the gang whose members smuggle cocaine and methamphetamine from Mexico into the United States for distribution. Florencia members are also involved in other criminal activities including assault, drive-by shooting, and homicide.
- Latin Kings: Latin Kings is a collection of over 160 structured gangs, referred to as chapters, operating in 158 cities in 34 states in the United States. The gang's membership is estimated to be 20,000 to 35,000. Most members are Mexican-American or Puerto Rican males whose main source of income is street-level drug sales. The gang obtains drugs primarily from Mexican drug trafficking organizations that operate along the U.S.-Mexico border. Members also engage in other criminal activity such as assault, burglary, homicide, identity theft, and money laundering.

Prison Gangs

According to federal law enforcement officials, prison gangs are criminal organizations that operate within federal and state prison systems as self- perpetuating criminal entities. These gangs also operate outside of prisons typically through the activities of members who have been released from prison into communities. Examples of prison gangs with transnational connections include the following:

- Barrio Azteca: Barrio Azteca is one of the most violent prison gangs in the United States. The gang is highly structured and has an estimated membership of 2,000. Most members are either Mexican national or Mexican American males. Barrio Azteca is most active in the southwestern United States, primarily in federal, state, and local corrections facilities in Texas and outside of prison in southwestern Texas and southeastern New Mexico. The gang's main source of income is derived from smuggling illegal drugs from Mexico into the United States for distribution both inside and outside prisons. Gang members often transport illicit drugs across the border for drug trafficking organizations. Gang members are also involved in other crimes including alien smuggling, arson, assault, extortion, kidnapping, and weapons violations.
- Hermanos de Pistoleros Latinos: This is a Hispanic prison gang formed in Texas in the late 1980s. It operates in most prisons in the state and on the streets in many communities in Texas, particularly Laredo. The gang is also active in several cities in Mexico, and its largest contingent in that country is located in Nuevo Laredo. The gang is structured and is estimated to have 1,000 members. These members maintain close ties to several Mexican drug trafficking organizations and are involved in the trafficking of large quantities of illegal drugs from Mexico into the United States for distribution.
- Mexican Mafia: This gang was formed in the late 1950s within the California prison system. It is loosely structured and has strict rules that must be followed by the estimated 350 to 400 members. Most of these members are Mexican American males who previously belonged to a Southern California street gang. Mexican Mafia is active in 13 states, but California remains the power base. The gang's main source of income is extorting drug distributors outside prison and distributing illegal drugs within the prison system and on the streets. Some members have direct links to Mexican drug trafficking organizations. Other criminal activities include controlling gambling and homosexual prostitution in prison.
- Mexikanemi: The Mexikanemi prison gang was formed in the early 1980s within the Texas prison system. The gang is highly structured and estimated to have 2,000 members, most of whom are Mexican national or Mexican American males who were living in Texas at the time of their incarceration. This gang poses a significant drug trafficking threat to communities in the southwest region of the United States, particularly Texas. Gang members reportedly traffic illegal drugs from Mexico into the United States for distribution inside and outside of prison. Gang members obtain these drugs from Mexican drug trafficking organizations.

- Surenos: As some individual Hispanic street gang members enter the prison systems, they put aside rivalries with other Hispanic gangs and unite under the name Surenos. The original Mexican Mafia members, most of whom were from Southern California, considered Mexicans from the rural, agricultural areas of Northern California as weak and viewed them with contempt. To distinguish themselves from these northern agricultural workers, members of Mexican Mafia began to refer to the Hispanic gang members that worked for them as Surenos (Southerners). Surenos gang members' main source of income is retail-level distribution of illegal drugs both within prison systems and in the community, as well as the extortion of drug distributors on the streets. Some members have direct links to Mexican drug trafficking organizations and broker deals for Mexican Mafia as well as their own gang. Other criminal activities of Surenos members include assault, car jacking, home invasion, homicide, and robbery.
- Texas Syndicate: Texas Syndicate is one of the largest and most violent prison gangs. It is active on both sides of the U.S.-Mexico border and poses a significant drug trafficking threat to communities in the southwest region. The gang is highly structured and is estimated to have 1,300 members, most of whom are Mexican American males between 20 and 40 years of age. Gang members smuggle illegal drugs from Mexico into the United States for distribution inside and outside of prison. Gang members have direct working relationships with drug trafficking organizations.

Outlaw Motorcycle Gangs

According to federal law enforcement, outlaw motorcycle gangs (OMG) have been in the United States longer than many other gangs and are most numerous in the United States. According to the Department of Justice (DOJ) Gang Unit, there are more than 300 active OMGs in the United States, ranging in size from single chapters with five or six members to hundreds of chapters with thousands of members worldwide. DOJ considers OMGs to be transnational criminal organizations because they typically maintain chapters in more than one country and engage in illicit cross-border activities. OMG chapters are found on every continent.

OMGs are highly organized with well-defined hierarchies, defined rules in the form of either bylaws or constitutions, and clear recruitment, acceptance, and promotion processes for members. OMGs have a distinct chain of command, much like a corporation with positions such as president, vice-president, treasurer, sergeant-at-arms, and road captain at the chapter level. Generally, OMG organizational structure consists of individual chapters grouped by geographic region all being headed by a national president. While national and international presidents may exist, each regional chapter is run by its own president. The gang leadership requires loyalty and obedience from members. OMG members may be governed by a code of ethics, a constitution, or a strict set of bylaws. Descriptions of major OMGs present in the U.S. follows—including details on the gangs' transnational connections.

- Hells Angels Motorcycle Club: According to U.S. law enforcement officials, the Hells Angels are the largest and the most criminally prominent of the "Big Five" OMGs.[49] The gang includes 2,000 to 2,500 members belonging to over 230 chapters in the United States and 26 foreign countries. In the United States, law enforcement officials estimate that Hells Angels has more than 92 chapters in 27 states with over 800 members. Gang members produce, transport, and distribute marijuana and methamphetamine and transport and distribute cocaine, hashish, heroin, and other drugs. Other crimes perpetrated by Hells Angels members include assault, extortion, homicide, money laundering, and motorcycle theft.
- Bandidos: U.S. law enforcement authorities consider the Bandidos and Hells Angels to be the two largest OMGs in the United States. This gang has approximately 900 members belonging to over 93 chapters in the United States, with a total of 2,000 to 2,500 members when the membership in 13 other countries is added to U.S. membership. Bandidos is involved in transporting and distributing cocaine and marijuana and producing, transporting, and distributing methamphetamine. The gang is most active in the Pacific, southeast, southwest, and west central regions of the United States and is expanding in these regions by forming new chapters and allowing members of support clubs[50] to form or join Bandidos chapters.
- Mongols Motorcycle Club: According to law enforcement officials, the Mongols Motorcycle Club is an extremely violent OMG that poses a serious criminal threat to the Pacific and southwest regions of the United States. Mongols members transport and distribute cocaine, marijuana, and methamphetamine and frequently commit violent crimes including assault, intimidation, and murder to defend Mongols territory and uphold its reputation. Most of the club's 300 members are Hispanic males who live in the Los Angeles area, and many are former street gang members with a long history of using violence to settle grievances. The club also maintains ties to Hispanic street gangs in Los Angeles. In the 1980s, the Mongols OMG seized control of southern California's OMG activity from the Hells Angels and today is allied with the Bandidos, Outlaws, and Pagan's OMGs against the Hells Angels.
- Outlaws: Outlaws has more than 1,700 members belonging to 176 chapters in the United States and 12 foreign countries. U.S. law enforcement officials estimate that Outlaws has more than 86 chapters in 21 states with over 700 members in the United States. Outlaws are the dominant OMG in the Great Lakes Region of the United States. Gang members produce, transport, and distribute methamphetamine and transport and distribute cocaine and marijuana. Other criminal activities engaged in by Outlaws include arson, assault, explosives operations, extortion, fraud, homicide, intimidation, kidnapping, money laundering, prostitution, robbery, theft, and weapons violations. Outlaws compete with the Hells Angels for membership and territory.
- Vagos Motorcycle Club: The Vagos OMG has hundreds of members in the United States and Mexico and poses a serious criminal threat to those areas in which chapters are located. Law enforcement reports that Vagos has approximately 300 members among 24 chapters in California, Hawaii, Nevada, Oregon, and three chapters in Mexico. Club members produce, transport, and distribute methamphetamine and distribute marijuana. Vagos members also have been implicated in other criminal activities including assault, extortion, insurance fraud,

money laundering, murder, vehicle theft, weapons violations, and witness intimidation.

- Black Pistons: This OMG is the official support club of the Outlaws Motorcycle Club. Established in 2002 with the backing of the Outlaws, Black Pistons has expanded rapidly throughout the United States and into Canada and Europe. The club has an estimated 70 domestic chapters in 20 states and an unknown number of foreign chapters in Belgium, Canada, Germany, Great Britain, Norway, and Poland. The exact number is unknown but is estimated to be more than 200 in the United States. The Outlaws OMG uses Black Pistons chapters as sources of prospective new members. The Outlaws also uses Black Pistons chapters to conduct criminal activity, especially transporting and distributing drugs. Black Piston members also engage in assault, extortion, fraud, intimidation, and theft.

Appendix III. Federal Agencies' Programs to Address Transnational Gangs with Connections to Central America

Federal agencies have developed and implemented a wide range of programs to combat transnational gangs in the United States that have links to Central America. As shown in table 4, some of these efforts directly combat the gangs while others seek to improve criminal justice systems to increase the ability of Central American countries to apprehend and prosecute criminals including gang members (such as Community Policing and Justice Sector Reform). As also shown in table 4, other efforts are aimed at improving educational and employment opportunities of youth to reduce the motivation for joining gangs (such as Youth Centers).

Table 4. Examples of Federal Efforts or Projects Implemented to Combat Central American Transnational Gangs, by Agency and Country Where Implemented

Lead implementing agency	Country	Effort or project	Description of effort/project
Federal Bureau of Investigation (FBI)	El Salvador	Transnational Anti-Gang Unit (TAG)	Through the TAG, information on MS-13 and 18th Street gang members is shared between U.S. law enforcement agencies and El Salvador's Civilian National Police for use in criminal inv-estigations and gang-member prosecut-ions. The TAG includes investigators from the Salvadoran police, Salvadoran prosecutors, and FBI agents. TAG fund-ing is provided by the State Department.
	Multiple countries in Central America	Central American Fingerprint Exploitation	This program collects biometric and fingerprint records maintained by Central American law enforcement agenc-ies and makes them accessible to U.S. law enforcement agencies. The progr-am helps countries acquire automated fingerprint technology along with tech-nical and other support. The system has been deployed in El Salvador, and ass-essments have been conducted in Belize and Panama and are planned for Guatemala and Honduras. Funding is provided by the State Department.
		MS-13 National Gang Task Force	To combat the transnational and natio-nal criminal activities of the MS-13 and 18th Street gangs, the FBI establis-hed this task force in 2005. The task force coordinates local, state, federal, and international FBI-led investigations of those gangs. It also manages the operation of the TAG.
		Central American Law Enforcement Exchange	This is an exchange program for law enforcement personnel from Central America and the United States to share best practices, establish contacts, and receive antigang training. The first exc-hange occurred with four gang officers from El Salvador's national police traveling to Los Angeles where they spent 30 days with gang officers of the Los Angeles Police and Sheriff's Departments. The Los Angeles officers subsequently visited El Salvador for 30 days. The FBI has modified the progam to a 3-week session that includes training at the FBI Academy. In the second exchange, which occurred in March 2009, 28 officers from the United States, El Salvador, Honduras, and Guatemala participated.
		Central American Intelligence Program	The objective of this program is to share intelligence, standardize reports and other intelligence products, and minimize the communication gaps bet-ween countries that allow gang memb-ers to operate across borders.

			The prog-ram is a joint initiative of the FBI and the State Department and consists of criminal-intelligence analysts from the United States, El Salvador, Honduras, Guatemala, Mexico, and Canada who work on gang-related matters.
		Criminal History Information Program	The FBI, in conjunction with U.S. Im-migration and Customs Enforcement (ICE), is working to implement this project to transmit the criminal histories to law enforcement authorities in El Sal-vador, Guatemala, and Honduras of deportees being returned to those coun-tries. Under this program, ICE is to pro-vide the FBI with a list of the criminals from these countries detained by ICE with final orders of removal. Next, FBI analysts compile the criminal histories of these detainees and transmit the info-rmation to law enforcement officials in each country. As of November 2009, the FBI was still in the process of hiring analysts and negotiating with the El Salvadoran government—the first country where the program will be implemented.
U.S. Immigration and Customs Enforcement (ICE)	Multiple countries in Central America	Electronic Travel Document System	This is an internet-based system to facilitate the issuance of travel documents for the removal of illegal aliens, including gang members. ICE has implemented the system in El Salvador, Guatemala, and Honduras.
		Operation Community Shield	This is an ICE initiative to combat transnational gangs by arresting and removing from the United States crimi-nal aliens who are gang members. ICE works with state and local law enforcement agencies to investigate transnational gang members who are foreign-born and in the country illegally or have been involved in crimes.
	Honduras	Operation Community Shield—Honduras	ICE established Operation Community Shield-Honduras in January 2010 in conjunction with the Department of State. This specialized law enforcement unit in
			Honduras represents ICE's first international antigang task force and consists of four Honduran National Police gang enforcement officers and one ICE Special Agent. This speciali-zed unit is charged with developing actionable gang intelligence to initiate and support current gang investigations in Honduras and the United States.
Department of State	El Salvador	Security Threat Intelligence Unit Program	The purpose of this initiative is to coll-ect, analyze, exploit and share gang intelligence within the prison system. According to the State Department, an effective intelligence program is essential in curtailing criminal activity both inside and outside the prisons since several thousand gang members, including much of the key leadership, are incarcerated throughout Central America.

	Multiple countries in Central America	U.S.- Central American Inte-gration System[a] Dialogue	This initiative includes talks between the United States and countries parti-cipating in the Central American Integ-ration System to promote regional coo-rdination against transnational threats such as criminal gangs.
		Antigang Training	This initiative provides training to Central American law enforcement officials through the U.S.-sponsored International Law Enforcement Academy in El Salvador. Training includes investigative techn-iques, prosecution, witness protection, rehabilitation, and management of gang members in prison. Participants have included police, prosecutors, judges, prison staff, border agents, and prevention and rehabilitation officials.
		Regional Corrections Advisor for Central America	The Regional Corrections Advisor serves as the regional corrections expert on the full range of corrections issues in Central America for the Department of State's Bureau of International Narcotics and Law Enforcement. The advisor coordinates corrections progra-ms with the Bureau of International Narcotics and Law Enforcement's Senior Corrections Advisor and the Regional Gangs Advisor for Central America. The advisor provides technical corrections expertise, policy guidance, technical assistance and training on behalf of the Bureau of International Narcotics and Law Enforcement for regional governments.
		Corrections Officer Exchange Program	Several state corrections departments have agreed to participate in this program for the identification and exchange of best practices with countries in the region.
U.S. Agency for International Development (USAID)	El Salvador	Justice Sector Reform	The purpose of this program is to prov-ide technical assistance and training to strengthen justice-sector institutions in El Salvador that will allow them to improve the investigation, prosecution, and prevention of crimes including those committed by gangs. The recipe-ents of USAID's assistance efforts include the El Salvadoran Attorney General and Public Defender's offices, the National Civilian Police, judges, and the courts.
		Dispute Mediation Centers Network	According to USAID, this program improves access to the justice system and promotes a culture of lawfulness and nonviolence by resolving conflicts through peer mediation. Through this program, USAID seeks to improve the reliability and effectiveness of the med-iation centers through training, techni-cal assistance, and public outreach. In implementing this program, USAID is working with the El Salvadoran Public Defender's Office, the Attorney General's Office, courts, schools, and selected municipalities. The program targets schools in areas with populations of students most at risk to be recruited to join gangs, in order to teach those youth how to resolve differences without resorting to violent practices or

			joining violent groups such as street gangs. USAID is also implementing a similar program in Nicaragua.
		Community-Based Crime and Violence Prevention Program	Under this program, USAID partners with local-government officials, community leaders, and private groups to develop prevention plans in selected municipalities at high risk for gang activity. Specifically, 10 high-risk comm-unities in five municipalities are parti-cipating in the development of crime prevention projects such as recreational infrastructure, sports activities, and vocational and arts centers.
		National Gang Prevention Policy	USAID provides technical assistance and training to strengthen El Salvador's National Council for Public Security to formulate national-level policy on gang prevention and coordinate prevention
			activities throughout the country. USAID intends for this program to inc-rease coordination between the national and local governments and bring toge-ther law enforcement officials, judges, and prosecutors to counter gangs and gang-related viole-nce. Beneficiaries of this program are the governmen t of El Salvador and selected municipalities throughout the country.
	Guatemala	Youth Centers	To reach at-risk youth, USAID started centers to provide a safe environment and access to sports activities and skills training. USAID is implementing this program through partnerships with faith-based organizations, the Rotary Club, nongovernmental organizations, and various municipalities.
		Youth Challenge Program	According to USAID, this program provides opportunities to develop new skills and offer free-time alternatives that reduce the vulnerability to gang recruitment for over 2,500 at-risk youth. This program builds on the results achieved under the Youth Alliance Program (responsible for "Youth Cen-ters" above) and seeks to open addit-ional centers and provide job placement to former gang members. This program partners faith-based organizations, the Rotary Club, small nongovernmental organizations, and municipalities.
		Community-Based Policing	USAID has sponsored this program in Villa Nueva, Guatemala, as part of an effort to reduce crime in the community—including crimes related to gang activity. According to USAID, the most important program activities include a diagnostic assessment to imp-rove the effectiveness of the national police, police training, and youth crime prevention activities—including those related to involvement with gangs. For example, the program facilitated a number of interventions that targeted youth at risk of joining street gangs. Recipients of assistance under this program include

			police, prosecutors, and members of the judiciary in addi-tion to the communities in which they all serve.
		24-hour Courts	According to USAID, the purpose of the 24-hour courts is to provide Increased
			efficiency in processing criminal cases—including those involving criminal gangs over which these courts have jurisdiction. This program is a joint effort of four justice institutions in Guatemala—courts, prosecutors, public defenders, and police.
		United Nations Commission against Impunity in Guatemala	Under this program, USAID supports the commission through direct funding and training of Guatemalan prosecutors and judges in the correct use of the law against organized criminal networks that have penetrated Guatemala.
		Crimes Against Life Unit	This program has provided for the reorganization of the Guatemala City Crimes Against Life Unit, procedural changes, and better case screening that has allowed the unit to increase prosecutions of homicides, including those related to gang violence.
		Desafio 100	According to USAID, this program is to help change public perception of reformed gang members. Desafio 100 provides a partnership between USAID and the business community in Guate-mala to provide 100 former gang members with jobs and special training.
		National Gang Prevention Policy	Under this program, USAID will prom-ote and assist Guatemalan institutions to develop and implement a national policy to institutionalize and promote sustainability of crime prevention programs for youth at risk of joining gangs. Participants in this program include the government of Guatemala and the judiciary.
	Honduras	Education for All	Under this program, USAID partners with the Honduran Ministry of Educa-tion, schools, communities, and other donors to provide education and voca-tional training for at-risk youth that will result in alternatives to joining gangs. Volunteer facilitators with diverse backgrounds implement the program at learning centers situated in factories, businesses, schools, and community centers throughout the country.
		Civil Rights and Values for Youth	USAID intends for this program to provide civic education and problem-solving skills for 20,000 at-risk youth from disadvantaged populations in Honduras. According to USAID, students are less likely to engage in criminal activities if they
			are educated in values and reintegrated into society. Program participants receive training in the fundamentals of civil society, volunteerism, a free-

			market economy, and democratic participation. USAID's program partners include nongovernm-ental organizations, Regional Ministry of Education Coordinators, Peace Corps volunteers, and other local partners in order to target vulnerable youth subject to violence, migration, gang recruitment, and school desertion.
		Municipal Conciliation Centers	USAID intends for this program to pro-mote crime and violence prevention through alternative dispute resolution. The program has set up seven centers throughout Honduras.
		National Gang Prevention Policy	Under this program, USAID partners with the Government of Honduras, local governments, the judiciary, and the private sector to develop a national policy framework for supporting municipal and community-led initiatives that address the root causes of gangs. These initia-tives include job placement and infrastructure projects that support community efforts to address root problems and improve security such as educational facilities, street lighting, and safer community spaces.
	Multiple countries in Central America	Regional Gang Prevention Program, Central American Region	The purpose of this program is to sup-port development of innovative gang prevention programs through small grants to various organizations. It will support public, private, and civil society organizations to implement gang prevention programs for at-risk youth and ex-gang members. This program address gang violence in three phases: (1) initiatives to prevent at-risk youth from joining gangs, (2) offer opport-unities to entice youth to leave gangs, and (3) rehabilitation efforts for ex-gang members to prevent them from returning to crime. Recipients of assi-stance under this program include the governments of Guatemala, El Salva-dor, and Honduras along with the judiciaries in these countries.

Source: GAO analysis of information provided by each applicable agency.

[a] The Central American Integration System is a regional entity created by Central American countries to, among other things, promote regional coordination against transnational threats such as criminal gangs.

Appendix IV. Federal Agencies' Entities and Mechanisms for Coordinating Transnational Antigang Efforts

Federal agencies have coordinated their programs to combat transnational gangs through working groups at the interagency level, coordinating groups within Central American countries, and federally led antigang task forces at the local level. For example, at the headquarters level, through the National Gang Intelligence Center (NGIC), representatives of the Department of Justice's (DOJ) Federal Bureau of Investigation (FBI); Drug Enforcement Administration (DEA); Bureau of Alcohol, Tobacco, Firearms, and Explosives (ATF); and Bureau of Prisons (BOP), among other components, and the Department of Homeland Security's (DHS) U.S. Immigration and Customs Enforcement (ICE) and U.S. Customs and Border Protection (CBP) coordinate and share information on gangs that are a threat to U.S. communities. Table 5 provides additional information about headquarters-level entities' coordination of antigang efforts. These coordinating entities have different roles and responsibilities, but in general, they serve as mechanisms for deconflicting cases;[51] providing law enforcement agencies with information on gangs and gang activities, including transnational gangs; and coordinating participating agencies' strategies and task forces.

In localities we contacted, law enforcement agencies obtained assistance from the antigang coordinating entities to support their investigations of MS-13 and 18th Street gangs and gang members. For example, in one location we visited, the National Gang Intelligence Center provided an analyst to an FBI antigang task force to help that task force analyze MS-13 gang data for an ongoing investigation. At another location, the FBI antigang task force obtained assistance from the TAG unit in El Salvador to help identify two MS-13 gang members who were in a Salvadoran prison and communicated with MS-13 gang members in the United States to direct the gang members' criminal activities. Additionally, DOJ's Gang Unit has assisted with the prosecution of MS-13 and 18th Street gang cases in the United States. For example, in one location we contacted, the Gang Unit assisted the local U.S. Attorney's Office with the prosecution of a gang case under the Racketeer Influenced and Corrupt Organizations Act.[52] The Gang Unit provided this assistance because, according to the U.S. Attorney's Office, the office did not have enough experienced attorneys who were familiar with using the Act to prosecute gang members. At the field level, federal law enforcement agencies utilize task forces to coordinate their gang enforcement efforts. For example, the FBI's Violent Gang Safe Streets Task Forces coordinate with federal, state, and local law enforcement to investigate all active gang threats, but have conducted investigations on MS-13 and 18th Street gangs across the country. In locations we contacted, including Omaha, Nebraska; Los Angeles, California; and Charlotte, North Carolina, FBI task forces investigated MS-13 gangs and determined that gang members in those locations were communicating with gang members in El Salvador.[53] Similar to the FBI's Violent Gang Safe Street Task Forces, ATF's Violent Crime Impact Teams, which partner ATF with federal, state, and local law enforcement agencies to reduce firearms-related violent crime including gang crime, may investigate gangs with transnational connections in specific locations.[54]

Table 5. Headquarters-Level Entities Focused on Coordination of Antigang Efforts

Entity	Year established	Lead agency or office	Participating agencies and offices	Staff	Coordination/ information-sharing role
Anti-Gang Coordination Committee	2006	DOJ Office of Deputy Attorney General	DOJ: FBI, ATF, U.S. Marshals Service (USMS), DEA, BOP, Executive Office for United States Attorneys (EOUSA), Office of Juvenile Justice and Delinquency Prevention, National Drug Intelligence Center, Civil Rights Division, Criminal Division, Office of Legal Policy, Budget Office, Office of Legislative Affairs, Office of Public Affairs, Justice Management Division, Office of Justice Programs, Attorney General's Advisory Committe e, Office of Community Oriented Policing Services, Tax Division, National Gang Targeting, Enforcement, and Coordination Center (GangTECC), NGIC, and National Institute of Justice DHS: ICE, CBP Department of the Treasury: Internal Revenue Service	None	Organize DOJ's efforts to combat gangs, including to provide recommendations to Deputy Attorney General on all matters related to antigang activities, review applications for funds for gang-related task forces from U.S. Attorneys and approve creation of violent-crime task forces around the country.
National Gang Intelligence	2005	DOJ FBI	DOJ: FBI, DEA, ATF, USMS, BOP, and National Drug Intelligence Center DHS: ICE, CBP	About 22, including a director, two deputy directors, 13 FBI	Provide law enforcement agencies with information and analysis of federal,

Table 5. (Continued)

Entity	Year established	Lead agency or office	Participating agencies and offices	Staff	Coordination/ information-sharing role
Center (NGIC)			Department of Defense: National Guard	intelligence ana-lysts, and at least one ana-lyst detailed from each participating agency	state, and local law enforce-ment intelligence focusing on gangs that pose a significant threat to U.S. communities.
National Gang Targeting, Enforcement, and Coordina-tion Center (GangTECC)	2006	DOJ Criminal Division	DOJ: FBI, DEA, ATF, BOP, USMS, and Criminal Division DHS: ICE	About 14, including a director, deputy director, and agents detailed from partici-pating agencies	Coordinate and deconflict ove-rlapping gang-related invest-tigations and prosecutions and serve as a coordinating center for multijurisdictional gang investigations.
MS-13 National Gang Task Force	2004	DOJ FBI	DOJ: FBI	Supervisor, four FBI supervisory special agents, and six FBI analysts	Coordinate the development of multijurisdictional FBI invest-igations of MS-13 and 18th Street gangs, including trans-national investigations, into national-level investigations and prosecutions.
Transnational Antigang unit (TAG)	2007	DOJ FBI	DOJ FBI, El Salvador's Civilian National Police	Two FBI agents 30 Salvadoran police officials and staff	Provide information on MS-13 and 18th Street gang mem-bers and their criminal active-ities in the United States and Central America. Information is shared between U.S. law enforcement agencies and the Salvadoran National Police. The TAG was created and implemented by the MS-13 National Gang Task Force to

Table 5. (Continued)

Entity	Year established	Lead agency or office	Participating agencies and offices	Staff	Coordination/ information-sharing role
					assist in combating the growing threat posed by transnational gangs and drug cartels in Central America.
Gang Unit	2006	DOJ Criminal Division	DOJ Criminal Division	12 prosecutors	Coordinate with local U.S. Attorneys' Offices on legal issues and multidistrict gang cases and work with law enforcement agencies to achieve coordinated prevention and enforcement strategies.

Source: GAO analysis of DOJ and DHS information.

For example, in 2007 ATF led an investigation in Baltimore, Maryland, involving MS-13 gang members who committed murder and robbery. Through its task force, ATF coordinated this investigation with other agencies including FBI, ICE, the United States Attorneys' Office, local police agencies, and the Salvadoran national police to investigate and prosecute these gang members. In addition, through Operation Community Shield, ICE works primarily with state and local law enforcement agencies to investigate gangs whose members are foreign- born or in the United States illegally, or both, or have been involved in crimes with a nexus to the U.S. borders.[55]

APPENDIX V. SCOPE AND METHODOLOGY

To determine to what extent the U.S. federal government has developed a strategy to combat transnational gangs with connections to Central America, we examined the interagency strategy, called the Strategy to Combat the Threat of Criminal Gangs from Central America and Mexico (the Strategy), and compared the contents of the Strategy to select criteria in our prior work on desirable characteristics of an effective national strategy, including (1) clear purpose, scope, and methodology; (2) discussion of problems, risks, and threats; (3) desired goals, objectives, activities, and performance measures; and (4) delineation of roles and responsibilities.[56] In regard to the National Security Council (NSC), we discussed its role in developing and implementing the Strategy with a mix of the departments and agencies that participated in the NSC's International Organized Crime Policy Coordinating Committee (IOCPCC) such as the Department of State (State), the Department of Justice (DOJ), and the U.S. Agency for International Development (USAID).[57] We also examined the roles and activities of the various federal agencies under the Strategy including DOJ, the Department of Homeland Security (DHS), State, the Department of Defense (DOD), the Department of the Treasury (Treasury), and USAID and their component agencies. To do this we reviewed antigang program documents and interviewed officials from DOJ, DHS, State, DOD, Treasury, and USAID in headquarters as well as component agencies such as the Federal Bureau of Investigation (FBI) within DOJ and U.S. Immigration and Customs Enforcement (ICE) within DHS to obtain their views about the framework, including the different categories, of the Strategy.

To determine how U.S. federal agencies have implemented programs to carry out the Strategy and combat transnational gangs, coordinated these programs, and assessed their results, we examined a mix of DOJ's, DHS's, State's, USAID's, and their component agencies' plans, performance data, reports, and assessments for fiscal years 2006 through 2009. We compared federal agencies' efforts to coordinate and share information on their transnational antigang programs to criteria in our prior work on effective interagency collaboration and results-oriented government.[58] To assess the reliability of statistical information we obtained, such as data on program performance and outcomes, we discussed the sources of the data with agency officials and reviewed documentation regarding the compilation of data. We determined that the data were sufficiently reliable for the purposes of this chapter. In addition, we examined federal agencies' funding allocated to transnational antigang programs. In particular, we reviewed agencies' budget requests for fiscal years 2008 through 2010; appropriations acts for DOJ, DHS, State, and USAID for those fiscal years;

and expenditure and other plans for the Mérida Initiative.[59] To obtain information on federal efforts to combat the gangs as well as the extent to which the agencies coordinated their efforts with other agencies, we interviewed a mix of federal, state, and local law enforcement officials in seven U.S. locations—Baltimore, Maryland; Charlotte, North Carolina; Laredo and McAllen, Texas; Los Angeles, California; Nashville, Tennessee; and Omaha, Nebraska—and U.S. federal, foreign, and three nongovernmental agencies' officials in El Salvador and Guatemala. To understand the process of how ICE handles and removes gang members who are in the United States illegally, we visited ICE's South Texas Detention Facility in Pearsall, Texas, and interviewed officials with ICE's Office of Detention and Removal Operations. We selected the U.S. locations and El Salvador and Guatemala based on a mix of criteria that included locations (1) along the U.S. borders, (2) where U.S. federal agencies have implemented antigang programs, and (3) where federal law enforcement agencies have conducted operations involving gangs with connections to Central America. For our site visits to foreign locations, we consulted with officials of federal agencies to identify in which foreign locations their agencies had efforts underway. Of the countries in the region, agency officials suggested we visit El Salvador and Guatemala because more antigang initiatives were underway and further along as compared to efforts in other countries. Given this, we selected these countries to obtain more information on these efforts and evaluate the effect they have had on the gang problem. We selected the South Texas Detention Facility because it was the facility identified by ICE officials for handling the most gang members awaiting removal. More specifically, in the U.S. locations we interviewed officials from some of the following federal agencies: the FBI; Bureau of Alcohol, Tobacco, Firearms, and Explosives (ATF); Drug Enforcement Administration (DEA); U.S. Attorneys' Office; ICE; and in Laredo, Texas, U.S. Customs and Border Protection (CBP). We also interviewed a mix of state and local law enforcement officials in Charlotte, North Carolina; Los Angeles, California; Nashville, Tennessee; and Omaha, Nebraska. In Guatemala and El Salvador, we interviewed a mix of officials from the following federal agencies: DOJ's Office of International Affairs, FBI, DEA; ICE; State; USAID; the State-sponsored International Law Enforcement Academy; and DOD. We also interviewed a mix of officials from Salvadoran and Guatemalan government agencies, including the countries' national police and the Salvadoran prosecutors' office. We also observed some of the activities related to USAID-sponsored prevention efforts in El Salvador and Guatemala such as the youth centers and interviewed participants, local government officials involved in the efforts, and members of the community about their views and the effect of the programs. Additionally, we interviewed officials from intergovernmental and nongovernmental organizations such as the Organization of American States, Washington Office on Latin America, the Central American Coalition for Prevention of Youth Violence, the Centro de Formacion y Orientacion, and the Instituto Universitario de Opinion Publica to obtain their perspectives on the gang problem in Central America. We also interviewed officials from contractors and companies such as Creative Associates International, Inc., and Pepsi Co. that have partnered with USAID or participated in USAID efforts to establish gang prevention programs and provide employment opportunities for ex-gang members in countries such as El Salvador and Guatemala. The information we obtained from interviewing officials in the U.S. and Central American locations cannot be generalized across all locations in the United States or Central America. However, because we selected these locations based on a variety of factors, they provided us with an overview of the agencies' antigang programs, examples of coordination and measurements to assess results, and any challenges with implementation of the programs.

We conducted this performance audit from April 2008 through April 2010 in accordance with generally accepted government auditing standards. Those standards require that we plan and perform the audit to obtain sufficient, appropriate evidence to provide a reasonable basis for our findings and conclusions based on our audit objectives. We believe that the evidence obtained provides a reasonable basis for our findings and conclusions based on our audit objectives.

APPENDIX VI. COMMENTS FROM THE DEPARTMENT OF HOMELAND SECURITY

U.S. Department of Homeland Security
Washington, DC 20528

Homeland Security

April 9, 2010

Ms. Eileen R. Larence
Director
Homeland Security and Justice Issues
U.S. Government Accountability Office
441 G Street, NW
Washington, DC 20548

Dear Ms. Larence:

RE: Draft Report GAO-10-395, Combating Gangs: Federal Agencies Have Implemented a Central American Gang Strategy, but Could Strengthen Oversight and Measurement of Efforts (Engagement Code 440702)

The U.S. Department of Homeland Security (DHS) appreciates the opportunity to review and comment on the draft report referenced above. The Government Accountability Office (GAO) makes two recommendations, one of which specifically is addressed to DHS.

The draft report recommends that the Attorney General and the Secretary of DHS reach agreement on the U.S. Immigration and Customs Enforcement's (ICE) role and participation in the joint U.S.-Salvadoran Transnational Anti-Gang (TAG) unit in order to strengthen federal agencies' coordination of anti-gang efforts and maximize use of federal law enforcement resources in El Salvador. We concur with the recommendation. Officials within ICE's Office of International Affairs, Office of Investigations and Office of Principal Legal Advisor have reviewed and revised the Federal Bureau of Investigation's (FBI) TAG memo to clarify ICE/FBI roles and responsibilities within the TAG in El Salvador. Currently a memorandum of understanding is being drafted.

The second recommendation is directed to the Special Assistant to the President for National Security Affairs. GAO recommends that the Special Assistant in conjunction with the Department of Justice, DHS, State, U.S. Agency for International Development, and the Department of Defense revise the *Strategy to Combat the Threat of Criminal Gangs from Central America and Mexico*. DHS officials defer to the Special Assistant to the President. DHS remains committed to assisting the Special Assistant and interagency partners in strengthening oversight and accountability for implementing the strategy and related revisions. This would include participating in a multi-agency oversight mechanism, which would use performance measures to report progress in implementation.

Technical comments have been provided previously under separate cover.

Sincerely,

Michael E. McFarland

for Jerald E. Levine
Director
Departmental GAO/OIG Liaison Office

APPENDIX VII. COMMENTS FROM THE DEPARTMENT OF JUSTICE

U.S. Department of Justice

Office of the Deputy Attorney General

Senior Counsel to the Deputy Attorney General
Chair of the Attorney General's Anti-Gang Coordination Committee

Washington, D.C. 20530

April 13, 2010

Eileen R. Larence
Director
Homeland Security and Justice Team
Government Accountability Office
441 G Street, NW
Washington, DC 20548

Dear Ms. Larence:

Thank you for the opportunity to review the U.S. Government Accountability Office (GAO) draft Report on Combating Gangs (April 2010) and for the opportunity to respond on behalf of the U.S. Department of Justice (DOJ). In the report, GAO recommends DOJ and the U.S. Department of Homeland Security (DHS) reach an agreement on the composition of an anti-gang unit located in El Salvador, and the roles of its members. DOJ fully agrees with this recommendation and has already taken steps to facilitate such an agreement.

As part of its gang strategy for the region, the FBI intends to create similar anti-gang units in Guatemala and Honduras. To strengthen federal agencies' coordination of anti-gang efforts and maximize use of federal law enforcement resources in the region, DOJ strongly believes that any agreement to ensure DHS's participation in the current unit, located in El Salvador, should also address its participation in the forthcoming units. We are working to reach this broader agreement for our anti-gang activities in the region.

Sincerely,

Jennifer Shasky Calvery

APPENDIX VIII. COMMENTS FROM THE UNITED STATES AGENCY FOR INTERNATIONAL DEVELOPMENT

USAID
FROM THE AMERICAN PEOPLE

APR - 9 2010

Ms. Eileen R. Larence
Director Homeland Security and Justice
U.S. Government Accountability Office
Washington, DC 20548

Dear Ms. Larence:

I am pleased to provide the formal response of the U.S. Agency for International Development (USAID) to the GAO draft report "Combating Gangs: Federal Agencies Have Implemented a Central American Gang Strategy, but Could Strengthen Oversight and Measurement of Efforts" (GAO-10-395, engagement 440702).

The enclosed USAID comments are provided for incorporation with this letter as an appendix to the final report.

Thank you for the opportunity to respond to the GAO draft report and for the courtesies extended by your staff in the conduct of this audit review.

Sincerely,

Drew W. Luten
Senior Deputy Assistant Administrator
Bureau for Management

Enclosure: a/s

U.S. Agency for International Development
1300 Pennsylvania Avenue, NW
Washington, DC 20523
www.usaid.gov

USAID COMMENTS ON GAO DRAFT REPORT No. GAO-10-395

USAID appreciates the GAO's thorough investigation of the question of U.S. Government interagency coordination to address the problem of crime and violence related to gangs operating between the United States and Central America. USAID is committed to furthering the U.S. Government's anti-gang strategy and welcomes the GAO's attention to these critical issues; in addition to its targeted anti-gang programming, USAID has long been engaged in institutional capacity building of the justice sector and violence prevention in Central America. We also appreciate the GAO's recognition of our efforts toward monitoring and impact evaluation of our anti-gang program, and acknowledge the importance of increased inter-agency coordination to bolstering USG efforts against the threat of criminal gangs both in Central America and within the U.S.

As the GAO noted, the gang problem is multifaceted, dynamic, and transnational in nature. As such, concerned actors continue to struggle with a dearth of reliable, accurate data on questions such as the numbers and demographics of gang members, or what percentage of crimes in Central America can truly be attributed to criminal gangs. This lack of reliable data presents a hurdle to measuring the overall impact of USG efforts to combat gang-related crime and violence. However, our progress has been significant. As noted in the report, USAID among others has helped to fill this information gap through activities such as the 2006 Central America and Mexico Gangs Assessment and our current efforts to measure impact of our Central American crime and violence prevention programs.

End Notes

[1] National Gang Intelligence Center and National Drug Intelligence Center, *2009 National Gang Threat Assessment* (Washington, D.C.: January 2009). The *2009 National Gang Threat Assessment* is a collaborative effort between the NGIC and the NDIC to examine the threat posed to the United States by criminal gangs. The assessment is based on federal, state, and local law enforcement information and is supplemented by information retrieved from open sources. Information and data used for that report were collected through September 2008. The NGIC is a multiagency effort that integrates the gang intelligence assets of federal, state, and local law enforcement entities to serve as a centralized intelligence resource for gang information and analytical support. The NDIC was established by the Department of Defense Appropriations Act, 1993, Pub. L. No. 102- 396, § 9078, 106 Stat. 1876, 1919 (1992). Placed under the direction and control of the Attorney General, NDIC was established to "coordinate and consolidate drug intelligence from all national security and law enforcement agencies, and produce information regarding the structure, membership, finances, communications, and activities of drug trafficking organizations." *Id.*

[2] MS-13 and 18th Street are Hispanic street gangs with members in both the United States and Central American countries. Throughout this chapter, we refer to "transnational gangs" as those gangs in the United States with connections to Central America. Appendix I provides additional information on MS-13 and 18th Street.

[3] The IOCPCC is an interagency committee of the NSC made up of various departments and agencies of the federal government such as DOJ, DHS, State, DOD, and USAID.

[4] GAO, *Combating Gangs: Better Coordination and Performance Measurement Would Help Clarify Roles of Federal Agencies and Strengthen Assessment of Efforts*, GAO-09-708 (Washington, D.C.: July 24, 2009).

[5] GAO, *Combating Terrorism: Evaluation of Selected Characteristics in National Strategies Related to Terrorism,* GAO-04-408T (Washington, D.C.: Feb. 3, 2004), and GAO, *Rebuilding Iraq: More Comprehensive National Strategy Needed to Help Achieve U.S. Goals*, GAO-06-788 (Washington, D.C.: July 11, 2006).

[6] GAO, *Results-Oriented Government: Practices That Can Help Enhance and Sustain Collaboration among Federal Agencies*, GAO-06-15 (Washington, D.C.: Oct. 21, 2005).

[7] The changes to immigration laws were included in two major pieces of legislation passed in 1996: The Illegal Immigration Reform and Immigrant Responsibility Act of 1996, Pub. L. No. 104-208, Div. C, 110 Stat. 3009-546 and the Antiterrorism and Effective Death Penalty Act of 1996, Pub. L. No. 104-132, 110 Stat. 1214. These laws expanded the offenses that constitute an "aggravated felony" rendering a noncitizen removable, and contracted available avenues of relief from removal.

[8] USAID, *Central America and Mexico Gang Assessment* (April 2006).

[9] SOUTHCOM is 1 of 10 unified combatant commands in DOD. It is responsible for providing contingency planning, operations, and security cooperation for Central and South America, the Caribbean (except U.S. commonwealths, territories, and possessions), and Cuba as well as for the force protection of U.S. military resources at these locations.

[10] The same U.S. Attorney serves the District of Guam and the District of the Commonwealth of the Northern Mariana Islands.

[11] Only federal laws specifically assigned to other divisions within DOJ are outside the purview of the Criminal Division. For example, a National Security Division was established in September 2006 with specific responsibility for international and domestic terrorism and other national security threats.

[12] The International Criminal Investigative Training Assistance Program was established in 1986 to help train police officers in Latin America. Its mission is to work with foreign governments around the world to develop professional and transparent law enforcement institutions that protect human rights, combat corruption, and reduce the threat of transnational crime and terrorism.

[13] The Office of Overseas Prosecutorial Development, Assistance and Training was established in 1991 to develop and administer technical assistance designed to enhance the capabilities of foreign justice-sector institutions and their law enforcement personnel to allow them to more effectively partner with DOJ in combating terrorism, trafficking in persons, organized crime, corruption, financial crimes, and other transnational crime.

[14] EOUSA provides operational support for information technology, training, and other functions, and prepares an annual statistical report of U.S. Attorneys, among other functions.

[15] INTERPOL is the world's largest international police organization, with 188 member countries. Created in 1923, it facilitates cross-border police cooperation, and supports and assists all organizations, authorities, and services whose mission is to prevent or combat international crime.

[16] Prevention refers to efforts to prevent, reduce, or minimize the incidence of gang activity and its negative consequences by dissuading at-risk youths from joining gangs. Intervention refers to efforts to support, encourage, and positively address the needs of individuals attempting to leave or who have left a gang, and may include efforts to persuade individuals to leave a gang.

[17] The initiative was named for the location of a March 2007 meeting between Presidents George W. Bush and Felipe Calderón of Mexico. The Mexican portion of the initiative is intended to complement U.S. and Mexican

domestic efforts against drug, human, and weapons trafficking. Subsequently, Congress added funding for Haiti and the Dominican Republic to address concerns about increased drug trafficking in the Caribbean.

[18] State has identified the following four strategic goals for the Mérida Initiative: (1) break the power and impunity of criminal organizations; (2) assist the governments of Mexico and Central America in strengthening border, air, and maritime controls; (3) improve the capacity of justice systems in the region; and (4) curtail gang activity in Mexico and Central America and diminish demand for drugs in the region.

[19] Pub. L. No. 110-252, § 1407(a), 122 Stat. 2323, 2340. Amounts appropriated for Mérida activities include those appropriated "to combat drug trafficking and related violence and organized crime, and for judicial reform, institution building, anti-corruption, rule of law activities, and maritime security." The act appropriated $65 million for assistance for the countries of Central America, Haiti, and the Dominican Republic, of which $2.5 million each was required to be made available for assistance to Haiti and the Dominican Republic.

[20] Pub. L. No. 111-8, § 7045(f), 123 Stat. 524, 887. Amounts appropriated for Mérida activities include those appropriated "to combat drug trafficking and related violence and organized crime, and for judicial reform, institution building, anti-corruption, rule of law activities, and maritime security."

[21] Consolidated Appropriations Act, 2010, Pub. L. No. 111-117, § 7045(f), 123 Stat. 3934, 3374 (2009). Amounts appropriated for Mérida activities include those available "to combat drug trafficking and related violence and organized crime, and for judicial reform, institution building, anti-corruption, rule of law activities, and maritime security." As described above, funds requested for Mérida activities were directed to be made available for CARSI. H.R. Rep. No. 111-366, at 1482 (2009) (Conf. Rep.).

[22] GAO, *Status of Funds for the Mérida Initiative*, GAO-10-253R (Washington, D.C.: Dec. 3, 2009).

[23] *See* H.R. Rep. No. 111-366, at 1482 (2009) (Conf. Rep.).

[24] *See* explanatory statement accompanying Consolidated Appropriations Act, 2008, Pub. L. No. 110-161, 121 Stat. 1844 (2007), at 1041 (noting that additional funding had been provided in the act "to enhance the unique Federal role ICE plays in investigating and disrupting organized transnational criminal gangs").

[25] The Strategy was announced at a July 2007 U.S.-Central American Integration System summit on security issues. The Central American Integration System is a regional entity created by Central American countries to promote regional integration. Among other things, one of the objectives of the system is to set up a new model of regional security and eradicate violence.

[26] According to State officials, U.S. embassies in Central America and Mexico and representatives from the Mexican and Central American governments also provided input to the development of the Strategy.

[27] GAO-04-408T and GAO-06-788.

[28] In prior work, to develop these desirable characteristics of an effective national strategy, we reviewed several sources of information. First, we gathered statutory requirements pertaining to national strategies, as well as legislative and executive branch guidance. We also consulted the Government Performance and Results Act of 1993, general literature on strategic planning and performance, and guidance from the Office of Management and Budget on the President's Management Agenda. In addition, among other things, we studied past reports and testimonies for findings and recommendations pertaining to the desirable elements of a national strategy. Furthermore, we consulted widely within GAO to obtain updated information on strategic planning, integration across and between the government and its partners, implementation, and other related subjects. For more information on how these characteristics were developed, see GAO-04-408T.

[29] GAO-04-408T and GAO-06-788.

[30] GAO, *Aviation Security: A National Strategy and Other Actions Would Strengthen TSA's Efforts to Secure Commercial Airport Perimeters and Access Controls*, GAO-09-399 (Washington, D.C.: Sept. 30, 2009).

[31] In addition to establishing performance measures for Mérida-funded programs in Central America, State plans to periodically discuss program results with countries in Central America. Specifically, under the terms of the agreements between the United States and the governments of each Central American country for implementing Mérida programs, representatives of each government will meet quarterly to evaluate the Mérida programs' progress toward achieving the performance measures described above.

[32] App. III provides a complete list of federal agencies' programs and efforts to combat transnational gangs with connections to Central America.

[33] When an alien is ordered removed from the Unites States, a consular official from the alien's country of origin must issue a travel document that allows the alien to return to his country. Once the alien's citizenship or nationality has been verified, the consular official issues a travel document to effect the alien's repatriation.

[34] The Integrated Automated Fingerprint Identification System is a national fingerprint and criminal history system maintained by the FBI. Incorporating gang members' criminal biometric data / fingerprint records from the Central American Fingerprint Exploitation should make the data/records accessible by all U.S. local, state, and federal agencies by means of this system.

[35] The first round of exchanges occurred in May 2008 with four gang officers from El Salvador's national police traveling to Los Angeles where they spent 30 days with gang officers of the Los Angeles Police and Sheriff's Departments. The Los Angeles--based officers subsequently traveled to El Salvador for 30 days. The FBI then modified the program to a 3-week session that includes training at the FBI Academy and other learning opportunities in Washington, D.C.; Los Angeles; and El Salvador. In March 2009, 28 officers from 11

different law enforcement agencies across the United States, El Salvador, Honduras, and Guatemala participated. In October 2009, 27 officers from law enforcement agencies in the United States, El Salvador, Guatemala, Nicaragua, and Panama participated.

[36] State's Bureau for International Narcotics and Law Enforcement Affairs funds the International Law Enforcement Academies. There are four academies, which are located in Europe (Budapest, Hungary), Southeast Asia (Bangkok, Thailand), Central America (San Salvador, El Salvador), and Southern Africa (Gaborone, Botswana); a regional training center in Lima, Peru; and a graduate-level academy (Roswell, New Mexico), in a cooperative effort with Treasury, DOJ, and DHS.

[37] "Deconfliction" is the coordination and information sharing among law enforcement agencies on multijurisdictional investigations to help ensure officer safety and the effective use of resources.

[38] GAO-09-708.

[39] As of March 2010, El Salvador is the only Central American country to host a TAG. The FBI is in the process of establishing another TAG in Guatemala in 2010. Although one has also been planned for Honduras, it has been postponed indefinitely due to political unrest in the country.

[40] According to ICE's country attaché, sometimes when special ICE enforcement operations ongoing in the United States result in a temporarily high volume of ICE requests for information, ICE has sent an agent on a temporary-duty basis to El Salvador to help the attaché process ICE requests and work with the TAG to fulfill the requests.

[41] GAO-06-15.

[42] Criminal arrests include aliens subject to removal who are charged with criminal violations, whereas administrative arrests refer to aliens who are unlawfully present in the United States but have not been charged with criminal violations.

[43] As of August 2009, FBI officials stated that establishment of a transnational antigang unit in Honduras has been placed on hold because of the political instability in the country.

[44] *See* Treaty of Extradition Between the United States of America and El Salvador, April 18, 1911, 37 Stat. 1516.

[45] We interviewed a mix of federal, state, and local law enforcement officials regarding MS-13 or 18th Street investigations in Los Angeles, California; Omaha, Nebraska; Nashville, Tennessee; Baltimore, Maryland; and Charlotte, North Carolina.

[46] USAID, *Central America and Mexico Gang Assessment* (Washington, D.C.: April 2006). This is the most recent regionwide assessment of gangs conducted by USAID.

[47] The Mexican Mafia prison gang operates mainly within the California Department of Corrections. It is loosely structured and has strict rules that must be followed by the estimated 350 to 400 members. Most members are Mexican American males who previously belonged to a Southern California street gang. The gang's main source of income is extorting drug distributors outside prison and distributing various narcotics within and outside the prison system. Some members of these prison gangs have direct links to Mexican drug trafficking organizations and broker deals for themselves and their associates. MS-13 and 18th Street are linked to numerous prison gangs, such as the Mexican Mafia, and these relationships are advantageous. Members must pay taxes to prison gangs in exchange for protection in prison. If members refuse, they risk being killed by the prison gangs.

[48] SOUTHCOM, Intelligence Assessment: Criminal Gang and Drug Trafficking: A Relationship of Convenience (March 13, 2008).

[49] The remaining four OMGs that make up the "Big Five" include the Bandidos Motorcycle Club (Bandidos), the Mongols Motorcycle Club (Mongols), the Outlaws Motorcycle Club (Outlaws), and the Pagans Motorcycle Club (Pagans).

[50] "Support clubs" are members of subordinate clubs that swear allegiance to a mother club and whose purpose is to do the "dirty work" of the mother club.

[51] "Deconfliction" is the coordination and information sharing among law enforcement agencies on multijurisdictional investigations to help ensure officer safety and the effective use of resources.

[52] While the Racketeer Influenced and Corrupt Organizations Act was originally enacted to dismantle organized crime groups such as the Mafia, prosecutors have successfully used it to bring cases against members of organized gangs. The Act prohibits the commission of a pattern of racketeering activity to invest in, maintain an interest in, or participate in, directly or indirectly, an enterprise, the activities of which affect interstate or foreign commerce; it also prohibits conspiracy to commit any of these activities. *See* 18 U.S.C. §§1961-68.

[53] The FBI's Violent Gang Safe Streets Task Forces are part of the FBI's Safe Streets Violent Crime Initiative which was designed to allow each field office to address violent street gangs and drug-related violence through FBI-sponsored task forces. The task forces were established in 1992 to serve as long-term and coordinated teams of federal, state, and local law enforcement officers and prosecutors. These task forces focus on disrupting and dismantling the most violent and criminally active gangs in the United States. According to the FBI, as of August 2009, 153 Safe Streets Task Forces are focused on violent gangs in 54 FBI field offices.

[54] ATF's Violent Crime Impact Teams were established in 2004 through partnerships with state and local agencies to reduce firearms-related violent crime including violent gang crime in small geographic areas experiencing

an increase in violent crime. According to ATF, as of April 2009, 31 Violent Crime Impact Teams were operating in locations across the country.

[55] ICE's Operation Community Shield was established in 2005 through partnerships with state and local law enforcement agencies as a national law enforcement initiative that targets violent transnational street gangs through the use of ICE's broad law enforcement powers to identify, locate, arrest, prosecute, and ultimately remove gang leaders, members, and associates from communities. Under this initiative, investigations focus on transnational street gangs whose members are subject to ICE's immigration and customs authorities because the members are foreign-born or in the country illegally, or both, or have been involved in crimes with a nexus to the U.S. borders (i.e., narcotics trafficking and human trafficking).

[56] GAO, *Combating Terrorism: Evaluation of Selected Characteristics in National Strategies Related to Terrorism*, GAO-04-408T (Washington, D.C.: Feb. 3, 2004), and GAO, *Rebuilding Iraq: More Comprehensive National Strategy Needed to Help Achieve U.S. Goals*, GAO-06-788 (Washington, D.C.: July 11, 2006). In addition to these four characteristics, our prior work identified two other characteristics which were outside the scope of our review: identification of future costs and resources needed and discussion of the strategy's integration with other strategies, entities, or efforts.

[57] During the course of our review, we attempted to meet with officials of the NSC to discuss the Strategy and its implementation, but were unsuccessful.

[58] GAO, *Results-Oriented Government: Practices That Can Help Enhance and Sustain Collaboration among Federal Agencies*, GAO-06-15 (Washington, D.C.: Oct. 21, 2005).

[59] Consolidated Appropriations Act, 2010, Pub. L. No. 110-117, 123 Stat. 3034 (2009); Omnibus Appropriations Act, 2009, Pub. L. No. 111-8, 123 Stat. 524; Supplemental Appropriations Act, 2008, Pub. L. No. 110-252, 122 Stat. 2323.

In: Transnational Gangs: The MS-13 Gang and Others
Editor: Michele L. Monteith
ISBN: 978-1-61728-917-0

Chapter 4

A CONTEMPORARY CHALLENGE TO STATE SOVEREIGNTY: GANGS AND OTHER ILLICIT TRANSNATIONAL CRIMINAL ORGANIZATIONS IN CENTRAL AMERICA, EL SALVADOR, MEXICO, JAMAICA, AND BRAZIL*

Max G. Manwaring

FOREWORD

In this monograph, Dr. Max Manwaring builds on his 2005 SSI monograph, *Street Gangs: The New Urban Insurgency*, and illustrates gang and Transnational Criminal Organization (TCO) linkage to instability and its aftermath. He explains that gang-generated instability leads to threats to national, regional, and global security, nation-state sovereignty, failing and failed states, and a "clash of civilizations." Thus, whether a gang or another TCO is specifically a criminal or an insurgent type organization is irrelevant. The putative objective of all these illegal nonstate entities—taken together, the analytical commonality that directly links gangs, TCOs, and insurgents—is to neutralize, control, or depose governments to assure their own commercial or ideological expectations. In this connection, gangs and their various possible allies (the gang phenomenon) are attempting to ensure that they have maximum freedom of movement and action within and between "sovereign" national territories. These objectives translate into more than an implicit political agenda.

The corrosive political effects of criminal violence along with the coerced assurance of freedom of action and movement also generate a kind of clash of civilizations. It is not a clash of western and eastern cultures. Rather, it is a clash between one set of values defined in terms of popular sovereignty and liberal democracy, and another set of values that has been characterized as criminal and feudal. Criminal values are derived from norms based on slave

* This is an edited, reformatted and augmented edition of a United States Strategic Studies Institute publication, dated December 2007.

holding, sexual activity with minors and their exploitation in prostitution, the farming of humans for body parts, and the killing and torture of innocents for political gain and personal gratification (as sport). This set of values is further denoted by patronage, bribes, kickbacks, cronyism, ethnic exclusion or exploitation, and personal whim. Thus, the ultimate threat of the destabilizing activities of the gang phenomenon is not violence, instability, the challenge to state sovereignty, or state failure. Instead, it is the coerced criminal imposition of a radical restructuring of the state and its governance.

This timely monograph contributes significantly to an understanding of a new kind of threat in which instability and irregular conflict are no longer on the political margins of the global security arena. For those responsible for making and implementing national security policy in the United States, the rest of the Western Hemisphere, and elsewhere in the world, this analysis is compelling. The Strategic Studies Institute is pleased to offer this monograph as a part of the growing interest in irregular war.

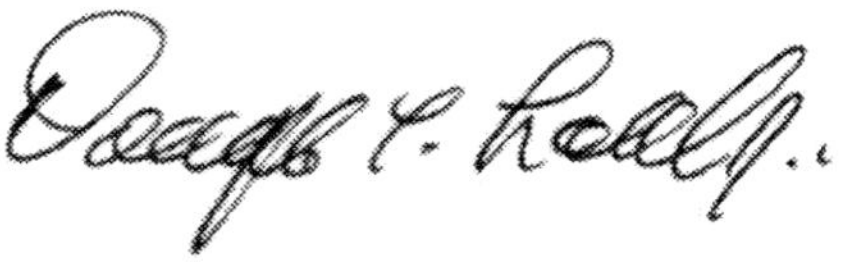

DOUGLAS C. LOVELACE, JR.
Director
Strategic Studies Institute

SUMMARY

Another kind of war within the context of a "clash of civilizations" is being waged in various parts of the Americas, Africa, Asia, Europe, the Middle East, and elsewhere around the world. Some of the main protagonists are those who have come to be designated as first-, second-, and third-generation street gangs, as well as their various possible allies such as traditional Transnational Criminal Organizations (TCOs). In this new type of war, national security and sovereignty of affected countries is being impinged every day, and gangs' illicit commercial motives are, in fact, becoming an ominous political agenda.

Rather than trying to depose a government with a major stroke (*golpe* or coup) or in a prolonged revolutionary war, as some insurgents have done, gangs and their allies (the gang phenomenon) more subtly take control of territory and people one street or neighborhood at a time *(coup d' street)* or one individual, business, or government office at a time. Thus, whether a gang is specifically a criminal or insurgent type organization is irrelevant. Its putative objective is to neutralize, control, or depose governments to ensure self-determined (nondemocratic) ends. This objective defines insurgency, a serious political agenda, and a clash regarding the authoritative allocation of values in a society.

The purposes of this monograph are to (1) introduce the gang phenomenon as a major nonstate player and a serious threat in the global and regional security arenas;(2) examine the gang phenomenon in Central America in general and in El Salvador, Mexico, Jamaica, and Brazil more specifically; and (3) summarize the key points and lessons and make brief recommendations. These cases demonstrate the analytical commonalities of various types of gang activities as they contribute to the instabilities that lead to the erosion of national security, nation-state sovereignty, the processes of state failure, and the struggle between democratic and criminal values.

Another kind of war (conflict) within the context of a "clash of civilizations" is being waged in various parts of the Americas, Africa, Asia, Europe, the Middle East, and elsewhere around the world.[1] Some of the main protagonists have been designated as first-, second-, and third-generation street gangs, as well as more traditional Transnational Criminal Organizations (TCOs), such as Mafia families, illegal drug traffickers, warlords, terrorists, insurgents, and so on. These gangs, and their various possible TCO allies, are not sending conventional military units across national borders or building an industrial capability in an attempt to "filch some province" from some country.[2] These illicit nonstate actors are more interested in commercial profit and controlling territory (turf) to allow maximum freedom of movement and action to achieve their longer-range objectives. The resultant freedom of action within countries and across national frontiers ensures commercial market share and revenues, as well as secure bases for controlling people, territory, and governments. The corrosive effects of the associated criminal violence and gratuitous cruelty, along with freedom of movement and action, also generate a clash of civilizations. It is not a clash of western and eastern cultures. Ultimately, it is a clash of controlling values between liberal democracy and criminal anarchy.[3]

What makes all of this into another type of contemporary conflict is that the national security and the effective sovereignty of affected countries are being impinged every day, and illicit motives are, in fact, becoming an ominous political agenda.[4] Rather than trying to depose a government in a major stroke (*golpe* or coup) or a prolonged revolutionary war, as some insurgents have done, gangs and their various possible allies slowly take control of national territory (turf) one street or neighborhood at a time (*coup d' street*) or one individual, business, or government office at a time. Thus, whether a gang's pursuit of freedom of movement and action is specifically commercial or ideological or a criminal or insurgent type of activity is irrelevant. The putative objective is to neutralize, control, or depose governments to ensure self- determined (nondemocratic) ends. This final objective defines insurgency, a serious political agenda, and a clash regarding the authoritative allocation of values in a society.[5]

The protean nature of gangs, organized crime, and contemporary insurgency does not accommodate conformity to any prescribed typology. Thus, I maintain the position I took in 2005—that is, the common denominator that defines gangs and other TCOs as mutations of insurgents is the unavoidable need to seize political power to guarantee the freedom of movement and action, as well as the ideological or commercial enrichment environments, desired. As a consequence, the "Duck Analogy" applies: when second- and third- generation gangs and other TCOs look like ducks, walk like ducks, and act like ducks—although they may be a peculiar breed—they are, nevertheless, ducks.[6] (Thus, hereafter, gangs and their various possible allies are referred to as the gang phenomenon.)

The purposes of this monograph, then, are to (1) introduce the gang phenomenon as a nonstate player and serious threat in the regional and global security arenas; (2) examine the gang phenomenon in Central America in general and in El Salvador and Mexico specifically; (3) examine different types of gangs in Jamaica and Brazil (as an addendum); and (4) summarize the key points and lessons and make brief recommendations, based on an examination of cases noted above. These cases demonstrate the analytical commonalities of various criminal gang activities as they contribute to the instabilities that lead to the erosion of nation-state sovereignty and the processes of state failure and the struggle between democratic and criminal values.

All this is designed to lead civilian and military leaders to the broad strategic vision necessary to begin to solve the next big set of security problems associated with the clash of controlling values in the 21st century. Strategic leaders must think about these problems from multiple angles, multiple levels, and in varying degrees of complexity.[7]

Context: Gangs as Nonstate Threats in the Regional and Global Security Arenas

The evolution of street gangs from small, turf- oriented, petty-cash entities to larger, internationalized, commercial-political organizations is often slow and generally ad hoc, depending on leadership and the desire and ability to exploit opportunities. Thus, gang violence develops from (1) the level of "protection," gangsterism, and brigandage; (2) to drug trafficking, smuggling people, body parts, armament, and other lucrative "items" associated with the global criminal activity; (3) to taking political control of ungoverned territory and/or areas governed by corrupt politicians and functionaries which can be uneven and incomplete. That is, most gangs never move beyond protectionism and gangsterism. Other gangs, however, act as mercenaries for larger and better organized criminal organizations. And as they expand their activities to compete with or support long-established TCOs, they expand their geographical and commercial parameters. Then as gangs operate and evolve, they generate more and more violence and instability over wider and wider sections of the political map and generate subnational, national, and regional instability and insecurity. Finally, as gangs evolve through these developmental and functional shifts, three generations emerge.

Three Generations of Gangs

First-Generation Gangs: Organization, Motives, and Level of Violence. The first-generation, or traditional, street gangs are primarily turf-oriented. They have loose and unsophisticated leadership that focuses on turf protection to gain petty cash and on gang loyalty within their immediate environs (for example, designated city blocks or neighborhoods). When first- generation street gangs engage in criminal enterprise, it is largely opportunistic and individual in scope, tends to be localized, and operates at the lower end of extreme societal violence—gangsterism and brigandage. Most gangs stay firmly within this first generation of development, but more than a few have evolved into and beyond the second generation.[8]

Second-generation Gangs. This generation is organized for business and commercial gain. These gangs have a more centralized leadership that tends to focus on drug trafficking and market protection. At the same time, they operate in a broader spatial or geographic area that may include neighboring cities and countries. Second-generation gangs, like other more sophisticated criminal enterprises, use the level of violence necessary to protect their markets and control their competition. They also use violence as political interference to negate enforcement efforts directed against them by police and other national and local security organizations. And, as they seek to control or incapacitate state security institutions, they often begin to dominate vulnerable community life within large areas of the nation-state.[9]

In this environment, second-generation gangs almost have to link with and provide mercenary services to TCOs and insurgents. As these gangs develop broader, market-focused, and sometimes overtly political agendas to improve their market share and revenues, they may overtly challenge state security and sovereignty. If and when they do, second- generation gangs become much more than annoying law enforcement problems. This point was made over 3 years ago in the following statement made by former El Salvadoran Vice-Minister of Justice Silvia Aguilar: "Domestic crime and its associated destabilization are now Latin America's most serious security threat."[10]

Third-generation Gangs. More often than not, elements of some gangs continue first- and second- generation activities while others expand their geographical bounds, as well as their commercial and political objectives. As they evolve, they develop into more seasoned groups with broader markets and a variety of allies. Additionally, second- and third-generation gangs are known to expand their activities—among others—to smuggling people, body parts, weapons, and cars; associated intimidation, murder, kidnapping and robbery; money laundering; home and community invasion; and other lucrative societal destabilization activities. As a consequence, they develop into sophisticated TCOs in their own right, with ambitious economic and political agendas.

In these terms, third-generation gangs inevitably begin to control ungoverned territory within a nation- state and/or begin to acquire political power in poorly governed space.[11] This political action is intended to provide security and freedom of movement for gang activities. As a consequence, the third-generation gang and its leadership challenge the legitimate state monopoly on the exercise of political control (authoritative allocation of values) and the use of violence within a given geographical area. The gang leader, then, acts much like a warlord, an insurgent leader, or a drug baron.[12] That status, clearly and unequivocally, takes the gang into mercenary activities, and intrastate war or nonstate war. Here, gang objectives aim to (1) neutralize, control, depose, or replace an incumbent government, (2) to control parts of a targeted country or sub-regions within a country and create autonomous enclaves that are sometimes called criminal free-states or parastates, and (3) in doing so, radically change the authoritative allocation of values (governance) in a targeted society to those of criminal leaders.[13]

Summary. First-generation gangs are traditional street gangs with a turf orientation. When they engage in criminal enterprise, it is largely opportunistic and local in scope. Second-generation gangs are engaged in business. They are entrepreneurial and drug-centered, and tend to pursue implicit political objectives. Third-generation gangs are primarily mercenary in orientation, and many of them seek to advance explicit political and social objectives. As such, third-generation gangs find themselves at the three-way intersection among crime, war, and politics; however, there is only one rule. That is, there are no rules (criminal anarchy).[14]

The Theoretical Conflict Terrain in which the Gang Phenomenon Operates

Before examining the characteristics of gangs and their links to other illicit transnational organizations, it is useful to sketch the basic outlines of the larger picture of the post-Cold War conflict situation and the place of the gang phenomenon in it. First, Dr. Steven Metz and Lieutenant Colonel Raymond Millen argue that four distinct but interrelated battle spaces exist in the contemporary security environment. They are: (1) traditional direct interstate war; (2) unconventional nonstate war; (3) unconventional intrastate war, which tends to involve direct vs. indirect conflict between state and nonstate actors; and (4) indirect interstate war, which entails aggression by a nation-state against another through proxies.[15]

Gangs and other nonstate actors operate most effectively in the second and third categories of nonstate battle space. Nonstate and intrastate wars involve political actors who thrive among and within various host countries. In describing the gang phenomenon as a simple mutation of a violent act that we label as insurgency, we mischaracterize the activities of nonstate players who are attempting to neutralize or take control of a state. We traditionally tend to think of insurgency as primarily a military activity, and we think of gangs and other TCOs as law enforcement problems. Yet, all these actors are engaged in a highly complete political act: "political war." This type of conflict is often called "irregular war," "insurgency war," "asymmetric war," "fourth-generation war," and "a complex emergency."[16]

This kind of war is defined as acting, organizing, and thinking differently from opponents to maximize one's own advantages, exploit an opponent's weaknesses, attain the initiative, and gain freedom of movement and action. In these terms, nonstate war exploits, directly and indirectly, the disparity between contending parties to gain relative advantage and uses terrorist and insurgent methods. Moreover, it can have political-psychological and physical dimensions, as well as lethal and nonlethal dimensions. Additionally, it can have both ideological-political objectives and commercial (search-for-wealth) motives, and it is constantly mutating.[17] As a consequence, there are no formal declarations or terminations of conflict; no easily identified human foe to attack and defeat; no specific territory to take and hold; no single credible government or political actor with which to deal; and no guarantee that any agreement between or among contending protagonists will be honored. In short, the battle space is everywhere and includes everything and everyone.[18]

In this context, the harsh realities of contemporary instability and chaos are caused by myriad destabilizers. The causes include increasing poverty, human starvation, widespread disease, and lack of political and socioeconomic justice. The consequences are seen in such forms as social violence, criminal anarchy, refugee flows, illegal drug trafficking and organized crime, extreme nationalism, irredentism, religious fundamentalism, insurgency, ethnic cleansing, and environmental devastation. These destabilizing conditions tend to be exploited by militant nationalists, militant reformers, militant religious fundamentalists, ideologues, civil and military bureaucrats, terrorists, insurgents, warlords, drug barons, organized criminals, and gangs working to achieve their own nefarious purposes. Those who argue that instability, chaos, and conflict are the results of poverty, injustice, corruption, and misery may well be right. We must remember, however, that individual men and women are prepared to kill and to destroy and to maim, and, perhaps, to die in the process, to achieve their self- determined ideological and/or commercial objectives. In the end, Zbigniew Brzezinski's reminder is useful: "Behind almost every [violent] act lurks a political problem."[19]

The Challenge and the Threat

A government's failure to extend a legitimate sovereign presence throughout its national territory leaves a vacuum in which gangs, drug cartels, leftist insurgents, the political and narco-right, and the government itself may all compete for power. In that regard, ample evidence clearly demonstrates that Central American, Mexican, Caribbean, and South American governments' authority and presence have diminished over large geographical portions of those regions.[20] However, contrary to popular perceptions, such areas are not "lawless" or "ungoverned." These territories are governed by the gangs, warlords, drug barons, and/or insurgents who operate where there is an absence or only partial presence of state institutions. In this sense, gangs' activities are not simply criminal and commercial in nature. For their own preservation and expansion, the second- and third-generation gangs—and sometimes even first- generation gangs—have little choice but to challenge the state either indirectly or directly. This unconventional type of conflict pits nonstate actors (gangs, warlords, drug barons, and/or insurgents) directly against nation-states and requires a relatively effective defense (military) capability.[21]

Tom Bruneau has identified five operational- level national security challenges associated with the transnational gang phenomenon:

- They strain government capacity by overwhelming police and legal systems through sheer audacity, violence, and numbers.
- They challenge the legitimacy of the state, particularly in regions where the culture of democracy is challenged by corruption and reinforced by the inability of political systems to function well enough to provide public goods and services.
- They act as surrogate or alternate governments in so-called ungoverned areas.
- They dominate the informal economic sector. They establish small businesses and use violence and coercion, and co-optation of government authorities, to unfairly compete with legitimate businesses.
- They infiltrate police and nongovernmental organizations to further their goals and in doing so demonstrate latent political aims.[22]

The gang challenge to national security, stability, and sovereignty and the attempt to neutralize, control, or depose governments takes us to the strategic-level threat. In this context, crime, violence, and instability are only symptoms of the threat. The ultimate threat is either: (1) state failure, or (2) the violent imposition of a radical socioeconomic-political restructuring of the state and its governance in accordance with criminal values. In either case, gangs contribute to the evolutionary state failure process by which the state loses the capacity and/or the will to perform its fundamental governance and security functions. Over time, the weaknesses inherent in its inability to perform the business of the state are likely to lead to the eventual erosion of its authority and legitimacy. In the end, the state cannot control its national territory or the people in it.[23]

However, just because a state fails does not mean that it will simply go away. (Haiti comes immediately to mind.) In fact, failing and failed states tend to linger and go from bad to worse. The lack of responsible governance and personal security generate greater poverty, violence, and instability—and a downward spiral in terms of development. It is a zero-sum game in which the gangs and the other nonstate protagonists involved are the winners, and the rest of the society is the loser. Additionally, the longer failing and failed states persist, the more they and their regional spillover effects endanger regional and global peace and security. Failing and failed states become dysfunctional states, rogue states, criminal states, narco-states, new "people's democratic republics," draconian states (for example, military or civilian dictatorships), or they reconfigure themselves into entirely new entities.[24]

Nevertheless, the foregoing possibilities do not delineate the end of the state failure problem. Sooner or later, the global community must pay the indirect social, economic, and political costs of state failure. The global community is increasingly expected to provide the military and financial leverage to ensure peace, security, and stability in an increasing number of post- conflict and unstable situations. The consistency of these lessons derived from relatively recent experience—from Asia's Golden Triangle to the Middle East, to Mexico, and from Central America to Haiti and the rest of the Caribbean Basin, to the White Triangle coca-producing countries of South America's Andean region—inspires confidence that these lessons and the associated threats are valid.[25]

The Gang Phenomenon in Central America, El Salvador, and Mexico

In the contemporary global security environment, governments, military and police forces, and other agencies responsible for various aspects of national security have little choice but to rethink security as it applies to "new" unconventional threats that many political and military leaders have tended to ignore or wish away. Probably the most significant unconventional threats facing leaders today are those generated by the gang phenomenon. The cases of the *Mara Salvatrucha* (MS-13) and the Eighteenth Street (*Mara*-18 or MS-18) gangs spreading from the United States, across Central America and Mexico, and into Europe illustrate the real impact of second and third-generation gangs functioning as networks with extensive transnational linkages.[26] Thus, this part of the monograph examines the strategic architecture of the gang phenomenon in Central America, El Salvador, and Mexico. That architecture focuses on motives and vision, organization and leadership, programs of action, and results.

The Basics of the Situation in Central America

The consensus among those who study this phenomenon is that many of the transnational gangs in Central America originated in Los Angeles, California, during the early 1990s. They were formed by immigrants whose parents had come to the United States to avoid the ongoing instability and violence in Central America during the 1980s. Once in the United States, many of the immigrants were exposed to and became involved with gangs in the rough neighborhoods where they grew up. The gangs began moving into all five Central American republics in the 1990s, primarily because convicted felons were being sent from prisons in the United States back to the countries of their parents' origins. These gangs include the famed MS-13, MS-18, other smaller gangs in El Salvador, and an estimated 63,700 kindred spirits in

Guatemala, Honduras, and Nicaragua.[27] It is noteworthy that the word *mara* is a slang term for "gang" and is derived from the name of a type of ant known for its ferocity. Literally, *trucha* means "trout" and is also a slang term for "shrewd Salvadoran." Thus, *Mara Salvatrucha* means a gang of shrewd Salvadorans.

What the Maras Do. Even though gangs in each country have some unique characteristics and can be bitter rivals for control of neighborhoods and other disputed territory or "turf," their origins, motives, and patterns of action are similar. These similarities begin with the various Central American gangs and their activities being intricately linked across international borders. Virtually all of them have flourished under the protection and mercenary income provided by larger and older TCO networks. The basis for those alliances is the illegal drug trade that is credited with the transshipment of 60 to 90 percent of the cocaine that enters the United States. In addition to trafficking in drugs, as noted above, Central American gangs are engaged in trafficking in human beings and weapons and are responsible for kidnappings, robberies, extortion, assassinations, and myriad other illicit, high- profit-generating activities.[28] On another level of activity, gangs are also engaged in intimidating and killing journalists, teachers, and candidates for political office who are not sympathetic to their causes.[29]

The root causes of gang activity in Central American countries and Mexico are also similar. They include gang members growing up in marginal areas with minimal access to basic social services; high levels of youth unemployment, compounded by insufficient access to educational and other public benefits; overwhelmed, ineffective, and often corrupt police and justice systems; easy access to weapons; dysfunctional families; and high levels of intrafamilial and intracommunity violence. Again, however, it is not poverty, injustice, or misery that willfully kill, maim, and destroy. It is individual men and women—and sometimes boys and girls—who are prepared to implement all kinds of horrible and coercive "intimidations" and "instabilities" in their personal search for status and well-being.[30]

Thanks to the activities of disaffected street gangs, overall crime rates have increased dramatically throughout the Central American region. Honduras has a murder rate of 154 per 100,000 population—double that of Colombia, even though that country is fighting three different insurgencies, as well as its various drug cartels. In El Salvador, the homicide rate is about 40 per 100,000 inhabitants; Guatemala's murder rate has risen 40 percent from 2001 to 2004 and is now approximately 50 per 100,000; and the murder rate in Mexico is estimated to be about 14 per 100,000. The Mexican figure is low by Central American standards but is considered "epidemic" by the World Health Organization (WHO). Additionally, as if these statistics were not grim enough, Mexico has the highest incidence of kidnapping in the entire world—with an estimated 3,000 kidnappings in 2004.[31]

The General Results of Gang Activity in Central America. The impact of gang violence on regional economies is significant. The Inter-American Development Bank (IDB) estimates the cost of violence throughout all of Latin America to be 14.2 percent of gross domestic product (GDP).[32] Despite the fact that the data required to calculate these costs is admittedly vague and inconsistent, the governments of all five Central American countries and Mexico have expressed serious concerns about transnational violence. For example, Belize, Guatemala, and Mexico have signed a multilateral agreement committing their governments to combating "narco-terrorism" and criminal gangs.[33] Guatemala and Mexico have gone a step further and signed multimillion dollar agreements with the United States to fight drugs and crime in those countries.[34] In the meantime, El Salvador and Honduras unilaterally continue to pursue hard-line anti-gang policies, including stronger law enforcement efforts and longer prison sentences.

Clearly, Central American gangs, their activities, and the impacts are linked across borders. As a result, an instability threat is definitely spilling from the region into neighboring countries. This is a regional problem that requires regional solutions, and for further analytical clarity, the two major gangs in El Salvador will be examined briefly.

El Salvador

As noted above, the roots of the *Maras'* presence in El Salvador are traced to Southern California in the 1980s and 1990s. In the aftermath of the 1992 Los Angeles riots, police determined that local gangs—including a little-known group of Salvadoran immigrant youth known as the *Mara Salvatrucha*—had carried out most of the looting and violence. In response, California passed strict, new anti-gang laws. Then, with the subsequent "three strikes and you're out" legislation of 1994, the prison population in that state increased dramatically. Additionally, in 1996, the U.S. Congress passed a "get tough" approach to immigration law. As a consequence of these successive pieces of legislation, thousands of convicted felons have been deported to El Salvador over the past several years. Significantly, until very recently, the Immigration and Naturalization Service's rules prohibited U.S. officials from informing El Salvadoran officials of the deportees' backgrounds.[35]

The results were disastrous for El Salvador. The deportees, also called "returnees," many of whom had never lived in El Salvador, arrived with their outlandish tattoos, their "Spanglish" language, and their arrogant attitudes. They quickly introduced the California gang culture, illegal drugs with their related "crack dens" and "crack babies," extortions, car-theft rings, burglaries, and contract killings. At first, Salvadoran officials had no idea what was happening—and when they began to understand the depth and seriousness of the problems brought by the gangs, they did not have the knowledge, experience, organization, or resources to deal with them. Given its momentum, the gang problem in El Salvador is thought to have escalated faster than in any other Central American country, and El Salvador now "is captive to the growing influence and violence of gangs."[36]

Organization. The two main gangs, MS-13 and MS- 18, boast 10,000 to 20,000 members. The Salvadoran National Council on Public Security estimates 39,000 members—22,000 in MS-13, 12,000 in MS-18, and another 5,000 in smaller gangs.[37] However, despite the lack of precise figures, these estimates are foreboding numbers in a country with a population of only 6.5 million. Like the estimated membership numbers, gang organization is not perfectly clear. Nevertheless, there appears to be a hierarchical pyramid structure that is common among Central American, Caribbean, and South American gangs.

At the top of the pyramid are the international bosses. Then, a second layer of international/transnational gang leadership exists. These second-level individuals oversee well-connected cells engaged primarily in trafficking global arms, drugs, and human beings. At the third level, gang cell members are involved in lower- level national vs. international trafficking of all kinds. Despite their national orientation, third-level members are in touch with upper-level as well as second- level members. This third level of gang membership contains centralized command and control elements that manage operational planning, finances, strategy, and provide some administrative support to the higher and lower echelons. Thus, they may be considered parts of a "Hollow Corporate Model." Additionally, national third-level gang cell members may manage geographically and functionally distributed "project teams."[38]

The fourth level of the generalized gang pyramid comprises the "neighborhood" gang members, a series of decentralized cliques (*clickas*) or cells responsible for specific neighborhoods or areas. Fourth-level individuals are not full-fledged MS-13 or MS-18 members. They make up three distinct levels at the lowest level of the gang pyramid—" sympathizers," "aspirants," and "nobodies," who do the drudge work in the *barrios* (neighborhoods/slums). They also act as mercenary "soldiers" for higher-level cells and project teams, or they may act as contracted mercenaries for other TCOs. As might be expected, this fourth-level group represents the largest segment of the total gang population, and their ages range from 8 to 18 years.[39]

Program of Action to Maximize Profits. The gangs' multilevel organization indicates a substantial enterprise, designed especially for conducting large- scale and small-scale business all the way from the transnational (global) level down to individual streets in specific *barrios* (neighborhoods) of El Salvador. This type of organization is also designed for quick and effective decisionmaking and decision implementation. In short, the first priority of the Salvadoran MS-13 and MS-18 gang organizations is operating a successful business, along with their own self-protection and promotion. More specifically, this type of organization permits continuous, protean operations over time. It allows for diversification of activities, diffusion of risk, and the flexibility to make quick adjustments and correct mistakes or exploit developing opportunities. The organization also provides a coherent mechanism for enforcing discipline and safeguarding operations at all levels. Additionally, it provides a planning facility that can deliberately expand or contract to adjust to drug, mercenary, other illicit operations, and to new allies, while increasing profits—depending on the requirements of each situation.[40]

These gangs have also become sophisticated enough to begin to prohibit specified members from getting new tattoos and to discipline severely (execute) members who break rules related to the consumption of crack and cocaine. All this indicates an evolution from first-generation well into second-generation gang status. Nevertheless, the current organization of MS-13 and MS-18 also reflects that these gangs maintain a first-generation focus on turf. The gang members at that level of evolutionary development operate under loose leadership, engage in a broad range of opportunistic, petty-cash-type criminal activity, and are often involved in serious intergang rivalry.[41]

The second-generation parts of the MS-13 and MS-18 organizations are interested in market protection and expansion and focus their illegal activities on drugs as a business. They are also known to engage in mercenary activities with various TCO partners. As the generalized pyramid organization suggests, the upper echelons are more cohesive, and leadership is more centralized. This second-generation group does not retain a specific turf orientation. Drug trafficking and mercenary activities become group rather than individual activities, and the gangs exploit both violence and technology to control their competition and absorb new markets. Thus, both generations of gang members currently exist within the overall organization. The turf part of the gang is more prevalent, but the "marketers" are more productive, wealthy, and powerful.[42] As MS-13 and MS-18 continue to evolve in their internationalization and sophistication, they are more and more likely to develop explicit political aims that truly threaten nation-states. This cautionary corollary takes us to the "Sullivan-Bunker Cocktail."

Results of Salvadoran Gang Activities. John Sullivan and Robert Bunker outline a pragmatic "cocktail mix" of nonmilitary methods by which a transnational nonstate actor, such as a second- or third-generation gang, can challenge the de jure security and sovereignty of a given nation. This "Sullivan-Bunker Cocktail" has proved to be the case in no less than 15 municipalities in El Salvador and in other political jurisdictions in neighboring Central American republics, Mexico, and Brazil.[43] Here is how it works:

> If the irregular attacker—criminal gangs, terrorists, insurgents, drug cartels, militant environmentalists, or a combination of the above—blends crime, terrorism, and war, he can extend his already significant influence. After embracing advanced technology weaponry, including weapons of mass destruction (including chemical and biological agents), radio frequency weapons, and advanced intelligence gathering technology, along with more common weapons systems, the attacker can transcend drug running, robbery, kidnapping, and murder and pose a significant challenge to the nation- state and its institutions.
>
> Then, using complicity, intimidation, corruption, and indifference, the irregular attacker can quietly and subtly co-opt individual politicians and bureaucrats and gain political control of a given geographical or political enclave. Such corruption and distortion can potentially lead to the emergence of a network of government protection of illicit activities, and the emergence of a virtual criminal state or political entity. A series of networked enclaves could, then, become a dominant political actor within a state or group of states. Thus, rather than violently competing directly with a nation- state, an irregular attacker can criminally co-opt and begin to seize control of the state indirectly.[44]

This is an example of a second-generation gang developing secure support bases through the application of coercive physical-psychological-political measures. In creating those secure support bases, gangs dominate local populations and erode the will of the system to resist their commercial enrichment efforts. This kind of "mix" of nontraditional activities is also a good example of a gang expanding its role while staying under the threshold of serious state concern and counteraction. Even though there may be no explicit political agenda, control of territory (turf) and the people in it are keys to the achievement of minimal goals. In these terms, gangs must eventually take, control, or neutralize political power to guarantee the kind of environment they want.

As a consequence, the gang nonstate actor evolves from second-generation toward third-generation status and represents a triple threat to the authority and sovereignty of a government and those of its neighbors. First, murder, kidnapping, intimidation, corruption, and impunity from punishment undermine the ability of the state to perform its legitimizing security and public service functions. Second, by violently imposing their power over bureaucrats and elected officials of the state, gangs and their allies compromise the exercise of state authority and replace it with their own. Third, by neutralizing (making irrelevant) government and taking control of portions of a given national territory and performing the tasks of government, the gang phenomenon can de facto transform itself into states within a state.[45] Accordingly, these parastates or criminal free-states "fuel a bazaar of violence where warlords and martial entrepreneurs fuel the convergence of crime and war."[46] And, the criminal leaders govern these areas as they wish.

Response to the Gangs. In 2003, El Salvador's Flores administration passed a hard-line (*mano dura*) law aimed at making it easier to jail gang members involved in criminal activity. However, that legislation was not considered to be strong enough. As a result, in 2004, new legislation was passed approving the new president's anti-gang program, called *Super Mano Dura* (Super Firm Hand or super hard line). This law provided stiffer penalties for gang membership—up to 5 years in jail for gang membership and up to 9 years for gang leadership. President Elías Antonio Saca's government reported that this "get tough" program reduced the number of murders that year by 14 percent. The following year, in 2005, new legislation tightened gun ownership laws and began a complementary effort of prevention and rehabilitation called *Mano Amiga* (Friendly Hand).[47]

The hard-line approach sent the message to the Salvadoran public that law enforcement is the only effective way to deal with the gang problem; thus, prevention and intervention (*Mano Amiga*) programs have received much less attention and fewer resources than are necessary to make them effective. Then, unanticipated second- and third-order consequences resulted in straining the capacities of the already overcrowded prison system. Moreover, the judicial and police systems became saturated; there were not enough properly trained personnel in those systems to manage the gang problem. By the end of 2005, a total of 12,073 prisoners were held in 24 prison facilities with a combined design capacity of 7,312. Since then, the gang problem has worsened significantly, and the only things Salvadoran leaders agree on are that prison provides a "graduate education" for gang members and that "something must be done."[48]

In sum, the Salvadoran government has not raised the level of the gang threat to the level of a threat to national security.[49] Nevertheless, from time to time since 2005, Army troops have been deployed to help the police patrol the streets.[50] Yet, to date, the *Maras* are still treated simply as a problem for law enforcement and the judicial system. In the meantime, the *Maras* control larger and larger parts of "turf" within the El Salvadoran national territory and effectively exercise their own sovereignty over the people in it. The *Maras* have thus evolved into an international network that extends from El Salvador, through Central America, to Mexico, the United States, and Europe.[51]

Mexico

Like Central America and El Salvador, Mexican authorities have no consistent or reliable data on the gang phenomenon in that country.[52] Nevertheless, the general public knows and acknowledges that the gang phenomenon in Mexico is large, complex, and convoluted. It also knows, first, that the gang situation is different in the South, along the Guatemala-Belize borders, from the situation in the areas between the southern and northern borders of Mexico, and the situation in the North, along the U.S. border. Second, it knows that, regardless of the accuracy of the data, a formidable gang presence exists throughout the country and—given the weaknesses of national institutions—considerable opportunities for criminality to prosper also exist.[53] As a result, the homicide rate along the northern and southern borders is considered epidemic, and Mexico has the highest incidence of kidnapping in the world. Clearly, violent gang and TCO activities in Mexico threaten the political development of the country.[54]

In the South, the El Salvadoran and other Central American *Maras* are positioned to negotiate the establishment of their own trafficking corridors through Mexico, and are strong enough to compete effectively with Mexican gangs. The *Maras* are also positioned to organize friendly or unfriendly takeovers of small cartels. As a result, *Maras* have made significant inroads into Mexican territory between the northern and southern borders, and have gained control of their own specified corridors through which illegal immigrants, drugs, weapons, and other illicit contraband are moved back and forth between the Guatemala-Belize border and the United States. As a consequence, it is reported that an *ad hoc* mix of up to 15,000 members of Mexican gangs and Central American *Maras* operate in more than 20 states.[55]

The key to the gang phenomenon in the North is the "Mexican Federation," a questionable (shifting) alliance of the "Big Four" (Juarez, Gulf, Sinaloa, and Tijuana) cartels. These cartels use the various gangs as temporary hired guns, and drug and contraband runners. Most of the gangs operating on the northern border of Mexico are long-time, well-established, "generational" (Mexican grandfathers, sons, and grandsons) organizations with 40- to 50-year histories. Reportedly 24 different gangs operate in the city of Nuevo Laredo, and 320 gangs operate within the city of Juarez, with an estimated total of 17,000 members in those two relatively small cities. The best-known gangs in the North are the Azteca, Mexicles, and Zeta organizations. Interestingly and importantly, the Central American *Maras* are also known to be used as mercenaries in the shifting alliances involving the northern drug cartels.[56]

With the aid of their various mercenary allies, the "Federation" is reportedly trying to negotiate, or force, a truce among its members regarding control of the lucrative transit routes that carry most of the cocaine consumed in the United States, as well as access into the rapidly developing domestic Mexican market. In the meantime, the various cartels and their gang allies continue to fight each other over territory or turf, and that fight is now extending into cyberspace.[57] To complicate matters further, there is the Mexican Mafia (La Eme or EME). At one time, all gangs operating south of Bakersfield, California, and into northern Mexico had to pay homage and take orders from the EME. That is no longer a rigid requirement. It is known, for example, that the MS-13 and MS-18 *Maras* broke that agreement as early as 2005.[58]

This convoluted array of Mexican gangs, Central American *Maras*, Mexican cartels, and the Mexican Mafia creates an almost anarchical situation throughout the country. As each gang and cartel violently competes and juxtapositions itself to maximize market share and freedom of movement and action, we see an operational environment characterized by the blurring of crime and war. In addition to outrageous violence and bloodshed, this environment is also creating small and large criminal-run "free-enclaves" in the cities and states of the Mexican nation-state. Moreover, the spillover transcends the supposedly sovereign borders of Mexico and its neighbors. This situation is similar in many ways to the medieval era, with feudal barons asserting total control over their fiefdoms. Violence and the fruits of violence—arbitrary political control—seem to be devolving to these small, private nonstate actors. This is a serious challenge to existing law and order in Mexico, to the effective sovereignty of that country, and to the security and sovereignty of the other nation-states within and between which the gang phenomenon operates.[59]

Organization and Motives. Mexican gangs and cartels are not homogeneous. There is no typology that applies to every one. Generally, however, power is migrating to the gangs and other TCO nonstate protagonists who can organize into sprawling networks more readily than traditionally hierarchical nation-state actors. These more horizontally organized criminal entities are among those evolving from the generalized pyramid structure into a flat, transnational organization that communicates and makes decisions instantaneously via cell phone and the Internet.

In this context, gangs and their TCO allies in Mexico, as in other countries, share many of the characteristics of a multinational Fortune 500 company. Thus, the phenomenon is an organization striving to make money, expand its markets, and move as freely as possible in the political jurisdictions within and between which they work. By performing its business tasks with super efficiency and for maximum profit, the general organization employs its chief executive officers and boards of directors, councils, system of internal justice, public affairs officers, negotiators, and franchised project managers. And, of course, this company has a security division, though somewhat more ruthless than one of a bona fide Fortune 500 corporation.[60]

The equation that links illegal narcotics trafficking to insurgency and to gangs in Mexico and elsewhere in the Western Hemisphere turns on a combination of need, organizational infrastructure development, ability, and the availability of sophisticated communications and weaponry. For example, the drug cartels possess cash and lines of transportation and communication. Gangs, insurgents, and paramilitary organizations have followers, organization, discipline, and arms. Illegal traffickers consistently need these kinds of people to help protect their assets and project their power within and among nation-states. Gangs, insurgents, and paramilitaries are in constant need of logistical and communications support—and money.[61]

The annual net profit from gang-related activities in Mexico is estimated to be in the billions of dollars. The precise numbers are not important, but the enormity of the amount of money involved is. Together with the additional benefits these financial resources can generate—when linked to utter ruthlessness and no moral or legal constraints—a second or third-generation gang can afford the best talent, whether lawyers, accountants, computer specialists, extortionists, murderers, or mercenary soldiers. At the same time, a gang can bribe government officials, hire thugs to intimidate (Mexico's high rate of kidnapping immediately comes to mind) those who cannot be bought, and kill those who cannot be intimidated. The profitable gang can also afford the best military and transportation equipment and communications technologies.[62] Deep pockets and flat organizational structure also mean that gangs and their TCO allies can move, shift, diversify, and promote operations quietly, subtly, and at will. Consequently, with these advantages, the phenomenon is known to have established status, acceptance, credibility, and de facto legitimacy in para-states (criminal free-states) within the Mexican nation-state.[63]

Where the Gang Phenomenon's Pursuit of Wealth Leads. Threats from gangs operating in Mexico come in many destabilizing forms and in a matrix of different kinds of challenges, varying in scope and scale. If these threats have a single feature in common, however, it is that they are systematic and well-calculated attempts to achieve implicit political ends. That is, the gang phenomenon creates political space from which to move and act without governmental or any other kind of hindrance. In this connection, we examine the erosion of Mexican democracy and the erosion of the nation-state. From there, we examine a corollary. We briefly look at political life in two emerging criminal free-states—Quintana Roo, on the southern border with Belize and Guatemala, and Sinaloa in the north.

The Erosion of Mexican Democracy. The policy- oriented definition of democracy that has been generally accepted and used in U.S. foreign policy over the past several years is best described as "procedural democracy." This definition tends to focus on the election of civilian political leadership and, perhaps, on a relatively high level of participation on the part of the electorate. Thus, as long as a country is able to hold elections, it is considered a democracy—regardless of the level of accountability, transparency, corruption, and ability to extract and distribute resources for national development and the protection of human rights, liberties, and security.[64]

In Mexico, we observe significant paradoxes. Elections are held on a regular basis, but leaders, candidates, and elected politicians are also regularly assassinated. As an example, literally hundreds of elected government officials who were considered unacceptable by the gangs and their allies have been assassinated following their election. Additionally, intimidation, direct threats, kidnapping, and the use of relatively minor violence on a person and/or his family play an important role *prior* to elections. As a corollary, it is important to note that although the media is free from state censorship, journalists and academicians who make their anti-narco-gang opinions known too publicly are systematically assassinated.[65]

Consequently, is hard to think of Mexican elections as being "democratic" or "free." Neither political party competition nor public participation in elections can be complete in an environment where armed and unscrupulous nonstate actors compete violently with legitimate political entities to control the government—before and after elections. Moreover, it is hard to consider Mexico as a democratic state as long as elected leaders are subject to corrupting control and intimidation that amount to informal vetoes imposed by unprincipled nonstate actors. As a consequence, David Jordan argues that Mexico is an "anocratic" democracy. That is, Mexico is a state that has the procedural features of democracy but retains the characteristics of an autocracy, in that the ruling elites (good or bad) face little or no scrutiny or accountability. Yet, regardless of definitions, the persuasive and intimidating actions of the gang phenomenon in the electoral processes have pernicious effects on democracy and tend to erode the will and ability of the state to carry out its legitimizing functions.[66]

The Erosion of the State. The Mexican state's ability to govern has undergone severe erosion on two general levels. First, the state's presence and authority are questionable over large geographical portions of the country. Second, the idea of the partial collapse of the state is closely related to the nonphysical erosion of democracy. Jordan argues that corruption is key in this regard and is a prime mover toward "narcosocialism."[67] In the first instance, the notion of partial collapse (erosion) refers to the fact that since the elections in 2000 and the political defeat of the previously all- powerful Institutional Revolutionary Party (PRI), state institutions in many of the rural areas and poorer urban parts of the country are absent or only partially present. Also, even in those areas that are not under the direct control of a gang-TCO alliance, institutions responsible for protecting citizens' security—notably the police and judiciary—have been intimidated and coerced to the point that they are unable to carry out their basic functions. Indicators of this problem are clear. The murder rate along the northern and southern borders of Mexico is among the highest in the world, accompanied by the grizzly and consistent murder and decapitation of police in those areas.[68] And, not surprisingly, there are never any witnesses to these atrocities.[69] These indicators of impunity strongly affirm that the state is not adequately exercising its social-contractual and constitutional-legal obligations to provide individual and collective security within the national territory.

In the second instance, nonphysical erosion of the state centers on the widespread, deeply entrenched issue of corruption. As one example, Jordan cites an interview given by an advisor to Mexico's attorney general under the administration of Carlos Salinas de Gortari. The advisor also served as president of Mexico's Association of Journalists and was a member of the executive committee of Mexico's Socialist Party. He stated, "The narcotics traffickers have penetrated not only the federal government, but the state governments and municipalities." In another interview, President Salinas's former secretary of finance stated, "It [the gang phenomenon] has penetrated the legislative, executive and judicial power of the country . . . [and it is] the most powerful economic organization in the world today, the world's most important multinational organization. . . . [The gangs and cartels have penetrated] all of the structures of power of Mexico, to the point that, without any euphemisms, the country does what the narco-traffickers want."[70] Clearly, the reality of corruption at any level of government favoring the gang phenomenon works against responsible governance and the public well-being. And, in these terms, the reality of corruption brings into question the reality of effective state sovereignty.

Thus, even though Mexico and the United States have recently signed an agreement on a $1 billion anti- narcotics assistance package,[71] Mexico's violent non- state actors remain strong and wealthy.[72] At the same time, as noted above, positive political sovereignty, democracy, socioeconomic development, territory, infra- structure, stability, and security are slowly being eroded. The real power of the gang phenomenon and the weakness of the state bring into question the wisdom and efficacy of providing corrupted Mexican institutions with the means to improve their effectiveness.

The Emergence of Criminal Free-States in Quintana Roo and Sinaloa. It appears that the gangs and cartels operating in these states have removed themselves from the constraints of Mexican state authority and replaced that authority with their own. Rather than competing directly with the state for political-economic dominance, the gang phenomenon has indirectly used corruption and co-optation to neutralize the state, as well as achieve secondary and tertiary objectives. The result is that Quintana Roo and Sinaloa have been viewed for a long time as "hotbeds of co-opted government and corruption [and] have become narcostates."[73] As a consequence, networks of government protection support those states' gangs and drug cartels. As one example, police protect drug shipments and other illicit commerce (humans) moving north to the U.S. market. Within this corrupt environment, levels of violence have increased due to co-opted factions of the police and enhanced employment of mercenaries.[74]

This corrupt environment affects everyone and everything, and has been described as feudal or medieval. Local gangs and their TCO allies have a safe haven from which to operate; enjoy immunity within that safe haven from any illicit actions; "tax" residents, travelers, and businesses at will; and maintain their own self-determined system of law and order. Actors in that world are known to derive their values from norms based on slave holding, sexual activity with minors and their exploitation in prostitution, the "farming" of humans for body parts, and the killing and torture of innocents for political gain and personal gratification (as sport). Notions such as due process of law, right to jury trial, individual privacy, and human and women's rights may exist as concepts among some, but do not appear to be practiced. Thus, in Quintana Roo and Sinaloa, people live in a feudal environment defined by patronage, bribes, kickbacks, cronyism, ethnic exclusion, and personal whim.[75]

Conclusions. The current situation in Mexico is more than a law enforcement problem. When gangs become de facto governments, they also become social actors. These social actors, who are also criminal-soldiers, are changing social, economic, and political organizations and violently "barbarizing" accepted values and modes of human behavior. A future vision of larger and larger parts of the global community adapting to criminal values and forms of behavior should be, at minimum, "unsettling."[76] In the meantime, the present vision of the human capacity to treat the gunshots and terrified screams from "down the street" as mere background noise to unexceptional every day life should create, at the least, a vague unease. This issue is more than a law enforcement problem, and it is more than a challenge to national sovereignty. This corrupt situation, and the barbaric criminal activities in it, take us back to the clash of civilizations' values.

The problems of stability, security, and effective sovereign governance in Mexico also take us back to, and beyond, the threat of state failure. State failure is a process—not an outcome. It is a process by which the state looses the capacity and/or the will to perform its legitimizing security and governance functions. It may also be a process by which the state is responding to the fact that it had never developed those capabilities in the first place.[77] In any event, ample evidence shows that the ultimate threat of destabilizing gang activities is not instability or criminal violence. It is not even state failure or the coerced imposition of a radical socioeconomic-political restructuring of the state and its governance.[78] Sooner rather than later, nations and international organizations will be forced to address the values that determine the *quality* of governance, security, and stability. One set of values serves cruel criminal greed. The other seeks the general well-being.[79]

A Hemispheric Addendum: Jamaican Posses (Gangs), and the Brazilian Primeiro Comando DA Capital

In addition to the *Maras* and other gangs in Central America and Mexico, hundreds more gangs operate in the Western Hemisphere. Two very different types of gang organizations may be found in Jamaica and Brazil. The various Jamaican posses are relatively homogeneous, violent, and ubiquitous. Interestingly and importantly, the Jamaican posses have also become a special set of social actors. They are making a social investment in the neighborhoods they control by performing some of the functions of the failing Jamaican "welfare state."[80] In contrast, one of the largest and most powerful gangs in Brazil, the Primeiro Comando da Capital (PCC), is not as interested in the well-being of the people it controls as it is in becoming "heroes (protagonists) without good or bad character—*heroes without any character*." These Brazilian protagonists' lack of ethics or moral principles surpasses even those of a citizen of the fictional Republic of Malandragem (that is, a bohemian outlaw). And, while these "heroes" do not seek to secede from the Brazilian state, they do seek to neutralize Brazilian politicians and make the state invisible and irrelevant.[81] Thus, Brazilian and Jamaican gangs fit the definition of ducks provided earlier. They are peculiar breeds to be sure but second and third-generation gangs, nevertheless.

Jamaican Posses (Gangs)

Similar to other countries in the Circum-Caribbean and elsewhere, Jamaican posses (gangs) are the byproducts of high levels of poverty and unemployment and lack of upward social mobility. Among other things, the posses also represent the consequences of U.S. deportation of Jamaican criminals back to the island and, importantly, of regressive politics in Jamaican democracy.[82] Unemployment and criminal deportation speak for themselves, but the political situation in Jamaica requires some elaboration.

Given the shift from the production of commodities toward knowledge-based products and services and reduction of the costs of transport, goods, and labor under economic "globalization," the Jamaican government has experienced a loosening of control of its traditional resource bases. As a result, the government no longer has the income to provide public services in a welfare-type state. When the Jamaican government provides public assistance, it has tended to "outsource" delivery of services to private and semiprivate organizations. Under these conditions, local posses have taken on a "social investment" in the areas they control. An important part of the posses' programs of action is called "shared government, with a welfare aspect."[83] As a result, gang-controlled communities in Jamaica are considered to be among the safest in the country, and the posses are helping the people in their "jurisdictions" with education, public health, and employment problems. Thus, as the state has reduced its traditional security and service functions, the gangs have stepped in to fill the vacuum and have become—among other types of social actors—social workers.[84] Nevertheless, it must be noted that the Jamaican posses remain deeply involved in serious intergang rivalry and violence. Their actions reflect on Jamaica not as a "failed state," but as a failing state in the process of reconfiguration. Thus, Jamaica appears to be slowly moving toward something like a "criminal state" or a "narco-state."

Organization. Posse members are primarily of Jamaican descent. It is estimated that there are at least 85 different posses operating on the island with anywhere between 2,500 to 20,000 members. Each posse operates within a clearly defined territory or neighborhood. The basic structure of a Jamaican posse is fluid but cohesive. Like most other gangs in the Americas, it has an all-powerful "don" or "area leader" at the apex of the organization, an upper echelon, a middle echelon, and the "workers" at the bottom of the social pyramid. The upper echelon coordinates the posse's overall drug, arms, and human trafficking efforts. The middle group manages daily operational activities. The lowest echelon performs street-level sales, purchases, protection, and acts of violence as assigned. When posses need additional workers, they prefer to use other Jamaicans. However, as posses have expanded their markets, they have been known to recruit "outsiders" as mules and street-level dealers, such as African-Americans, Trinidadians, Guyanese, and even Chinese immigrants. They are kept ignorant of gang structure and members' identities. If low-level workers are caught, the posse is not compromised; if they are not, the revenue continues to come in.[85]

Program. Jamaican posses are credited with being self-reliant and self-contained. They have their own aircraft, watercraft, and crews for "pick up and delivery" and their own personnel to run legitimate businesses and conduct money-laundering tasks. In that connection, posses have expanded their operations into the entire Caribbean Basin, the United States, Canada, and Europe. The general reputation of Jamaican posses is one of high efficiency and absolute ruthlessness in pursuit of their territorial and commercial interests. Examples of swift and brutal violence include but are not limited to fire bombing, throat slashing, and dismemberment of victims and their families. As such, Jamaican posses are credited with the highest level of violence in the English-speaking Caribbean and 60 percent of the crime in the region.[86]

This example of gang activity fits very well into the typological description of second-generation gangs evolving toward third-generation status. They are organized for business and commercial gain. They have a more hierarchical leadership structure than more politically oriented, security-conscious, and flatly organized third-generation gangs. Members tend to focus on drug trafficking, with market protection a first concern and market expansion second. They use the level of violence they consider necessary to protect their markets and control their competition. Violence is their political interface to negate law-enforcement efforts directed against them by police and other security organizations. And, as they seek to control or incapacitate national and international security institutions, they dominate community life, territory, and politics. In this environment, posses are forced to link with and provide services to other posses and to other illicit transnational organizations from time to time.[87]

Domination of posses' respective turf in Jamaica's confined area makes constant cooperation and negotiation with other gangs, TCOs, and the state conditions for generating the degree of stability necessary to conduct profitable business. That kind of cooperation was demonstrated in May 2006 with a month-long series of civic activities called a "Safe Communities Campaign." This government initiative's purpose was to assist selected communities—and the posses in them—to think and act in terms of reggae icon Bob Marley's message of "love, peace, and unity."[88] When these kinds of efforts fail, however, the results are conflict and a level of violence commensurate with the level of importance of the issue(s) involved. In that context, one can see the rise of private, don-controlled enclaves that coexist in delicate, often symbiotic, relationships with the Jamaican government and its security institutions. Thus, as one kind of authority has withdrawn from a given turf, another has moved to fill the vacuum. That, in turn, blurs the line between criminal and political violence and gives the posses increasing immunity to state intervention and control.[89] As other consequences, the effective sovereignty of the state and the personal security of citizens are being challenged every day, and the posses' commercial motives for controlling people and territory are, in fact, an implicit political agenda.[90]

The Jamaican case is almost a classic example of first- through third-generation gang activity and development. The generic evolution of urban street gangs illustrates that this is a compound-complex issue with implications at three different levels of analysis. First, all three generations of gangs generate serious domestic instability and insecurity. Of course, as gangs evolve, they generate more and more violence and instability over wider and wider sections of the political map and create regional instability and insecurity. Second, because of their internal (intrastate) criminal activities and their international (transnational) commercial and political alliances and actions, they exacerbate the confusion regarding traditional distinctions between police law enforcement functions and military national security functions. Thus, very little that is effective or lasting has been done to control or eliminate them. Third, when first-, second-, and third-generation gangs or parts of gangs dominate a country's political stage at one level or another, they erode the effective sovereignty of the nation-states within and between which they operate.[91]

Response. Within the context of that frustration, some contemporary civilian, military, and police leaders appear to have recognized that this modern global world is much too interrelated, complicated, and dangerous to advocate a strictly law-enforcement solution—or even a strictly military solution—to provide any viable response to local and regional security, stability, and sovereignty threats. The argument is that what is required is a unified civil-military effort to apply the full human and physical resources of the nation-state, as well as the international community, to generate effective multilateral solutions to transnational issues.[92] A good example of such a holistic, multidimensional, and multilateral approach is the cooperation for security that was achieved between and among the English-speaking states in the Circum-Caribbean during the April-May 2007 World Cricket Matches.[93]

Apart from the personal and collective security provided by the cooperation of the international community at the 2007 Cricket Matches, however, the Organization of American States (OAS), the United States, and the various Caribbean governments have been unable or unwilling to deal effectively with the gangs that permeate the region. The OAS affirmed in 2003 that gang-related "threats, concerns, and other challenges are cross-cutting problems that may require hemispheric cooperation" and that "the traditional concept and approach [to security threats] should be expanded to encompass new and nontraditional threats. . . ." The final result of this affirmation was the *condemnation* of "transnational organized crime, since it constitutes an assault on institutions in our states and negatively affects our societies."[94] Even so, the OAS has been reluctant to go beyond its diplomatic "condemnation." The United States has not done much more. To be fair, however, it must be noted that for 2006, the United States put $10 million into the ongoing antidrug and anticrime efforts outlined in the "Third Border Initiative" (that is, the U.S. "third border" that includes the Gulf of Mexico and Caribbean areas) and is providing other benefits under the Caribbean Basin Initiative.[95] Given the entire scope of the issue, however, this level of funding is clearly not enough.

Conclusions. The democratically elected governments in the Caribbean argue that criminal gangs, such as the Jamaican posses, have been able to profit from their globalized operations to the point of succeeding in placing themselves beyond the capability of most of the mini-countries in the region to destroy them or even seriously disrupt their operations. Today it is estimated that any given gang-cartel combination earns more money in a year from its illicit activities than any Caribbean country generates in legitimate revenues. Thus, individual mini-state governments in the region are simply overmatched by the gang phenomenon. The gangs and their various allies have more money, better arms, and more effective organizations than the states. And, gangs are gradually supplementing the brute violence of previous generations with the brainpower of a new generation of members who are computer savvy and business-school trained with MBAs. Additionally, many of this younger generation of gang members, like the older generations, are recipients of "graduate educations" from North American and other prison systems.

In all, increasing gang effectiveness, violence, and impunity have fueled doubts in the Jamaican citizenry about the problem-solving ability of their elected leaders.[96] Given the reality of the posses' combination of power and beneficial social welfare activities, citizen support and allegiance tend to go to the posses that deliver consistent services and security, rather than to the government that appears to be unable or unwilling to honor the social contract.

The Brazilian Primeiro Comando da Capital

The great city of São Paulo, Brazil—the proverbial industrial "locomotive" that pulls the "train" of the world's eighth largest economy—was paralyzed by the Primeiro Comando da Capital (PCC) for 5 days in mid-May 2006. Virtually nothing moved. More than 293 attacks on individuals and groups of individuals were reported, and hundreds of people were killed and wounded. Busses were torched, banks were robbed, personal residences were targets of violence, municipal buildings and police stations were attacked, and rebellions broke out in 82 prisons within the state of São Paulo's penal system. Transportation, businesses, factories, offices, banks, schools, and shopping centers were shut down. In all, the city of São Paulo was a frightening place during those 5 days in May.[97]

During that time, the PCC demonstrated the ability to coordinate simultaneous prison riots; destabilize a major city; manipulate judicial, political, and security systems; and shut down the formal Brazilian economy. The PCC also demonstrated its complete "lack of principles" through its willingness to indiscriminately kill innocent people, destroy public and private property, and suspend the quality of life benefits of a major economy for millions of people. Beyond the severe limitations of the state government's security forces—which were reportedly as involved in extra-judicial killings as the criminal perpetrators of the chaos—the violence and chaotic conditions in São Paulo made any effort to assert governmental authority or conduct essential public services virtually impossible.[98]

Organization and Motives. The PCC has an estimated 65,000 to 125,000 full- and part-time dues-paying members and is led by a brilliant and uncompromising career criminal called Marcola (Marcos Williams Herbas Camacho). Although analysts believe that no more than 6,000 active PCC members are in Brazil's prison system, they know that the PCC has extended its influence into the *favelas* ("ungoverned" slums)[99] in São Paulo, Rio de Janeiro, and the other major cities of the country. This has been accomplished through a long series of carefully negotiated, sometimes forced alliances with other gangs and *favela* chiefs (*jefes da favela*).[100] As a result, at any given time, Marcola controls at least 60,000 PCC members in the prisons and *favelas* of Brazil. And, notably, the May explosion in São Paulo was initiated, orchestrated, and terminated by one person—Marcola—from a "maximum security prison," using his mobile telephone.[101]

Ostensibly, this turmoil and retribution was triggered by prisoners who were being transferred to a maximum security prison that was not equipped to allow the inmates to watch the much anticipated World Cup soccer matches on TV. Thus, an ambitious, prisoner-initiated "prison rights" agenda was the motive for the rebellion. But, at its base, consensus has it that the "surprise May explosion" in São Paulo was really a show of force by the largest criminal gang in the Western Hemisphere. The primary intent was to announce to the state and federal governments that the PCC and its allies in the *favelas* are strong enough to compel the negotiation of terms of state sovereignty vis-à-vis that organization.[102] Unlike many gangs in the hemisphere that seek to permeate government to the point where the state authorities and selected gang members are the same people, the PCC has attempted to neutralize the Brazilian state within its sphere of influence. At the least, given that Marcola got everything he wanted out of the negotiations to end the chaos in São Paulo, it is probably safe to say that the PCC and the *jefes* or barons of the *favelas* have grown more and more powerful, and the state increasingly constrained.[103]

Program of Action. Favelas are the base of the PCC's extended power. In the *favela*, "traffic" is everything, and "territory controlled" is critical. The PCC, like other criminal gangs throughout the hemisphere and the world, is deeply involved in drug trafficking, arms trafficking, murder, kidnapping, robberies, and extortion. To maintain its momentum and expand its markets, the organization has increasingly adopted an offensive mode with tactics appropriate to urban guerrilla war, in which it looks for confrontations with rival gangs and police and military forces. PCC members and temporary-hire "soldiers" from the *favelas* carry out their violent tasks armed with automatic weapons, machine guns, hand grenades, rocket propelled grenades, anti-personnel mines, and crudely armored vehicles. Command and control is provided primarily through a very efficient communication network based on mobile telephones. This takes us back to Marcola and his cell phone. In areas controlled by the PCC or in areas that might be "invaded" by PCC-controlled units, one has a choice: to pay dues, mentally submit, and physically contribute to the organization or "*subir al cielo*" (to die).[104]

In addition to its violent turf-controlling efforts and illicit trafficking activities, the PCC pursues more than a casual, self-serving criminal rights agenda. The organization hires from 18 to 20 lawyers who work full- time. They not only act as advocates for gang members, but also act as mentors for young people. One of the great successes of the PCC has been to infiltrate or "colonize" the governmental organization that administers the entrance examinations necessary to enter the Brazilian public service. The job of the PCC mentor is to ensure that young gang members who have the ability and the desire to enter into public service can and do get their necessary education and pass the appropriate examinations. As a consequence, the PCC is preparing to put its own people into bureaucratic positions it considers important in the Brazilian system. Thus, in addition to controlling slums in the major cities of the country, the third-generation parts of the PCC appear to be slowly and surely extending their influence into the public service. The logical conclusion regarding this effort would be, simply, that Marcola is deliberately leading his organization to infiltrate the state.[105] This, of course, would be an important objective in the process of securing freedom of movement and action and in moving Brazil toward criminal-state status. This would also be a radical variation on the previously noted Sullivan-Bunker cocktail.

Response. It would appear that the São Paulo state government and the Brazilian federal government were not particularly concerned with the specific issues that brought on the May 2006 crisis. The official state of São Paulo response to the violence and chaos was simply: "I say to our people the police are still in the streets, they [the people] can go out and have fun this weekend."[106] This "business (or fun) as usual" approach to the gang problem and to the ungoverned territory issue is similar to that expressed not too long ago when a high-ranking federal official said: "Not to worry. Brazil will grow out of this."[107]

On the positive side of this dilemma, the unfortunate São Paulo 2006 "explosion" brought to light socioeconomic-political-psychological problems—poverty, corruption, penetration of the political system, and impunity—that probably will be debated sooner rather than later. It is hoped that such debates will result in more than simply "tough talk." In that connection, the Brazilian people are demonstrating their displeasure with the "business as usual" (official lassitude, inefficiency, and outright corruption) approach to dealing with the PCC and other gangs.

On the negative side, several points must be made. First and most seriously, vigilante militias are violently beginning to impose their own "peace" in *favelas* the police do not control.[108] Second, the governor of the state of Rio de Janeiro has authorized shows of force of his own. As one example, he ordered the state police, backed by a federal task force, to invade and take control of a notorious drug-trafficking slum (the Complexo do Alemão) in June 2007. It was a brutal and bloody effort, the police were not particularly selective regarding who they killed, and human rights advocates were outraged.[109] Interestingly, the people of Rio (Cariocas), presumably those who do not live in the *favelas*, appear to have approved of that police action. As a matter of fact, the individual who planned the raid was subsequently singled out at a public event and given a hero's ovation.[110]

Third, a truce, enforced by 25,000 federal troops, police from several Brazilian states and international police organizations, cooperatively worked to turn Rio de Janeiro into a relatively safe and peaceful city during the period up to and after the prestigious Pan American Games in July 2007. Reportedly, Cariocas "rejoiced" as the usual hectic pace of murder, assault, and theft slowed to almost negligible proportions. Brazil's President Luiz Inácio Lula da Silva responded to public pressure and announced that 75 percent of the military and police equipment brought into Rio during the games would remain in the city.[111] How that equipment will be used over time remains to be seen, but Cariocas have been reminded what it feels like to live in a safe city.

Conclusions. In the meantime, the June 2007 episode of police violence in Rio and the 2006 violence organized by Marcola and the PCC in São Paulo illustrate that loosely governed states and ungoverned territories within them are attractive venues for gangs and other nonstate actors who seek to avoid the reach of criminal justice systems and evade surveillance and sanctions. Lessons from these experiences also illustrate that effective action against gangs requires close civilian- military and international-national-local partnerships.

The May 2006 incident in São Paulo is a prime example of a "new urban jungle," within which gangs and their warlord and insurgent cousins can find space from which to conduct their illicit, commercial enrichment operations.[112] Ironically, Marcola and his fellow PCC prisoners in the São Paulo penal system have found a safe place for conducting their unprincipled, second-generation gang move toward third-generation status. This mixing of commercial and political interests is a lethal combination that exemplifies a real and significant threat to the security, stability, and effective sovereignty of the Brazilian state. The São Paulo and Rio experiences also reinforce the most salient strategic-level lesson learned from the Cricket Matches and the Pan American games. That is, gang and other criminal activities are transnational, intrastate problems requiring cooperative transnational and intrastate solutions.

Implications

It appears that commercial enrichment remains the primary motivation for gang challenges to state security and sovereignty in the Western Hemisphere. The primary objective, however, is to *indirectly* ensure that the gang phenomenon has the level of freedom to act within and between national territories that allows the achievement of the desired commercial enrichment. In these terms, gangs and their allies are not *directly* challenging incumbent governments for control of the state. By responding to this kind of challenge to sovereignty in traditional ways, including accepting corrupt practices and/or pretending the problem will go away, most political leaders are playing into the hands of the gangs. They do not appreciate the nature and extent of the violent challenge to political order and the values of legitimate governance being raised by the gang phenomenon.[113]

The power to deal with these kinds of threats is not hard combat firepower or even more benign police power. It involves soft, multidimensional, multilevel, multilateral, political, psychological, moral, informational, economic, and social efforts, as well as police and military activities that can be brought to bear holistically on the causes and consequences, as well as the perpetrators of violence. Ultimately, then, success in contemporary unconventional conflict comes as a result of a unified effort to apply the full human and physical resources of the nation-state and its international allies to achieve the individual and collective well-being that can lead to sustained societal peace.[114]

Key Points and Lessons

What makes the above cases or situations and their implications significant beyond their own domestic political context is that they are situations from which lessons from contemporary irregular warfare can be learned. Additionally, these cases are the results and harbingers of much of the ongoing political chaos of the 21st century. They stress the following:

- Gangs and other TCOs contribute significantly to national, regional, and global instability. As they evolve, they generate more and more terror, violence, and instability over wider and wider sections of the political map.
- Gangs, along with their TCO allies, are far from being apolitical and unique. They are becoming more and more similar to their politicized insurgent and warlord cousins. They maintain a practical logic regarding conflict that is a continuation of regional politics by other means.

- The primary motives of gangs and other TCOs center on group survival and personal gain. Beyond this there are no rules (criminal anarchy).
- Gangs and other TCOs use completely unprincipled political-psychological, as well as purely violent ways and means to achieve their objectives.
- These objectives are, primarily, freedom of movement and action within and across national boundaries. The unintended or intended results impinge on the effective sovereignty and security and liberal democratic values of countries and peoples.
- The civil-military relations problem regarding the question of whether or not the gang phenomenon is a law enforcement issue or a national security issue is irrelevant. It is larger than that. It requires the application of all the instruments of power of the nation-state and its international allies.
- To dismiss the above realities as too difficult or impossible to deal with is to accept the inevitability of unattractive alternatives.

Sun Tzu reminds us that we do not need an abundance of manpower, specialized equipment, and financial resources to deal effectively with an enemy such as the protean gang phenomenon: "What is of supreme importance in war is to attack the enemy's strategy... and his plans....Next best is to disrupt his alliances."[115] This kind of effort does not require several pages of "actionable" and "measurable" tactical-operational hard power recommendations or more equipment and training or more money for the salaries for "civil servants"—although all that would be helpful. Sun Tzu's winning strategic-level soft power recommendations to attack the enemy's strategy, plans, and alliances require, more than anything else, the well-considered application of "brain power." The alternative for the United States is to watch the Western Hemisphere become further engulfed in a chaos of vice, corruption, lack of legitimacy, and criminal values.

Biographical Sketch of the Author

MAX G. MANWARING holds the General Douglas MacArthur Chair and is Professor of Military Strategy at the U.S. Army War College. He is a retired U.S. Army colonel and an Adjunct Professor of International Politics at Dickinson College. He has served in various civilian and military positions, including the U.S. Army War College, the U.S. Southern Command, and the Defense Intelligence Agency. Recently he published *Uncomfortable Wars Revisited* (University of Oklahoma, 2006). Dr. Manwaring is the author and coauthor of several articles, chapters, and reports dealing with political-military affairs, democratization and global ungovernability, and Latin American security affairs. He is also the editor or co-editor of *El Salvador at War; Beyond Declaring Victory and Coming Home: The Challenges of Peace and Stability Operations*; *Deterrence in the 21st Century*; and *The Search for Security: A U.S. Grand Strategy for the Twenty-First Century*. Dr. Manwaring holds a B.S. in Economics, a B.S. in Political Science, an M.A. in Political Science, and a Ph.D. in Political Science from the University of Illinois. He is also a graduate of the U.S. Army War College.

End Notes

[1] For early discussions of these phenomena, see Samuel Huntington, *The Clash of Civilizations and the Remaking of World Order*, New York: Simon & Schuster, 1996; and Robert D. Kaplan, *The Coming Anarchy*, New York: Random House, 2000. Also see David Easton, *A Framework for Political Analysis*, Englewood Cliffs, NJ: Prentice-Hall, 1965; and David Easton, *The Political System: An Inquiry into the State of Political Science*, Chicago: University of Chicago Press, 1971, 1981.

[2] Carl von Clausewitz, *On War*, Michael Howard and Peter Paret, trans. and eds., New Brunswick, NJ: Princeton University Press, 1976, p. 596.

[3] Huntington, 1996; and Kaplan, 2000. Also see Easton, 1965; and Easton 1971, 1981.

[4] John P. Sullivan, "Terrorism, Crime and Private Armies," *Low IntensityConflict& Law Enforcement* , Winter 2002, pp. 239-253; John P. Sullivan and Robert J. Bunker, "Drug Cartels, Street Gangs, and Warlords," in Robert J. Bunker, ed., *Nonstate Threats and Future Wars*, London: Frank Cass, 2003, pp. 40-53; Max G. Manwaring, *Street Gangs: The New Urban Insurgency*, Carlisle, PA: Strategic Studies Institute, U.S. Army War College, 2005.

[5] *Ibid.* Also see Easton, 1965; Easton 1971, 1981.

[6] Manwaring, 2005.

[7] Easton, 1965; Easton 1971, 1981. David Easton formulated and elaborated the concept of "authoritative allocation of values" as the accepted definition of politics.

[8] Sullivan and Bunker, 2003.

[9] *Ibid.*

[10] Statement made at a U.S. Army War College/Florida International University (USAWC/FIU) conference entitled "New Security Threats in the Western Hemisphere," held at Washington, DC: The Center for Strategic and International Studies (CSIS), June 29, 2004.

[11] Sullivan and Bunker, 2003.

[12] John Mackinlay, "Warlords," *Defence and International Security*, April 1998, pp. 28-32. Also see John Mackinlay, *Globalization and Insurgency*, London: The International Institute for Strategic Studies, 2002.

[13] John Mackinlay, "Beyond the Logjam: A Doctrine for Complex Emergencies," in Max G. Manwaring and John T. Fishel, eds., *Toward Responsibility in the New World Disorder*, London: Frank Cass, 1998, pp. 114-131. Also see Sullivan and Bunker, 2003.

[14] John P. Sullivan, "Maras Morphing: Revisiting Third Generation Gangs," *Global Crime*, August-November 2006, pp. 488-490.

[15] Steven Metz and Raymond Millen, *Future Wars/Future Battle Space: The Strategic Role of American Landpower*, Carlisle, PA: Strategic Studies Institute, U.S. Army War College, 2003, pp. ix, 15-17.

[16] Paul E. Smith, *On Political War*, Washington, DC: National Defense University Press, 1989, p. 3.

[17] Steven Metz and Douglas V. Johnson, II, *Asymmetry and U.S. Military Strategy: Definitions, Background, and Strategic Concepts*, Carlisle, PA: Strategic Studies Institute, U.S. Army War College, 2001, pp. 5-6. Also see Steven Metz, *The Future of Insurgency*, Carlisle, PA: Strategic Studies Institute, U.S. Army War College, 1993, pp. 13-15; and Steven Metz and Raymond Millen, *Insurgency and Counterinsurgency in the 21st Century: Reconceptualizing Threat and Response*, Carlisle, PA: Strategic Studies Institute, U.S. Army War College, 2004, p. 15.

[18] A very sobering and interesting analysis of this type of conflict may be found in *Unrestricted Warfare*, Beijing: PLA Literature and Arts Publish House, 1999, p. 109.

[19] Zbigniew Brzezinski, *The Choice: Global Domination or Global Leadership*, New York: Basic Books, 2004, p. 28. Also see Max G. Manwaring, *The Inescapable Global Security Arena*, Carlisle, PA: Strategic Studies Institute, U.S. Army War College, 2002, p. 7.

[20] *Ibid.*

[21] *Ibid.*; also see Francisco Rojas Aravena, "Nuevo contexto de seguridad internacional: nuevos desafíos, nuevas oportunidades?" ("The New Context of International Security: New Risks and New Opportunities?"), in Francisco Rojas Aravena, ed., *La seguridad en América Latina pos 11 Septiembre*, Santiago: and Arturo Contreras Polgatti, *Conflicto en la* , Santiago: Mago Editores, 2004.

[22] T. C. Bruneau, "The Maras and National Security in Central America," *Strategic Insights*, Vol. 4, Issue 5, 2005.

[23] Daniel C. Esty, Jack Goldstone, Ted Robert Gurr, Barbara Harff, and Pamela T. Surko, "The State Failure Project: Early Warning Research for U.S. Foreign Policy Planning," in John L. Davies and Ted Robert Gurr, eds., *Preventive Measures: Building Risk Assessment and Crisis Early Warning Systems*, New York: Rowman & Littlefield, 1998.

[24] Chester A. Crocker, "Engaging Failed States," *Foreign Affairs*, September/October 2003, pp. 32-44; Stephen D. Krasner and Carlos Pascual, "Addressing State Failure," *Foreign Affairs*, July/August 2005, pp. 153-163.

[25] The author has conducted a series of interviews with more than 300 senior U.S. and Latin These interviews took place from October 1989 through July 1994, September 1996, December 1998, November 2000, February 2001, March 2002, February 2003, March and August 2004, and March through May 2006. To allow

anonymity for those who have objections to their names being made public, these are cited hereafter as Author *Drugs and Security in the Caribbean: Sovereignty under Siege*, University Park, PA: Pennsylvania State University Press, 1997; W. Lee Rensselaer III, *The White Labyrinth*, New Brunswick, NJ: Transaction, 1990; and Luis Bustamente Belaunde, y discomposición the State"), in Federico R. Leon and Ramiro Castro de la Mata, eds., *Pasta Basica de Cocaina, abuso de drogas* (*Coca Paste and Cocaine: The Abuse of Drugs*), Lima: CEDRO, 1990, pp. 301-321; Stephen E. Flynn, *The Transnational Drug Challenge and the New World Order*, Washington, DC: Center for Strategic and International Studies, 1993; and David C. Jordan, *Drug Politics: Dirty Money and Democracies*, Norman, OK: University of Oklahoma Press, 1999.

26 Bruneau, 2005.

27 "Central America and Mexico Gang Assessment," Washington, DC: U.S. Agency for International Development, Bureau for Latin America and Caribbean Affairs, April 2006, hereafter referred to as AID Paper, 2006.

28 Ana Arana, "The New Battle for Central America," *Foreign Affairs*, November/December 2001, pp. 88-101; Ana Arana, "How the Street Gangs Took Central America," *Foreign Affairs*, May/June 2005, pp. 98-110; Oscar Bonilla, "Current Situation of Gangs in El Salvador," unpublished paper written for the Consejo Nacional de Seguridad Pública del Salvador, November 2004.

29 *Ibid.*; also see Mark Lacey, "Drug Gangs Use Violence to Sway Guatemalan Vote," *The New York Times*, August 4, 2007, at www.nytimes.com/2007/08/04/world/Americas/04guatamals.html.

30 AID Paper, 2006; also see Manwaring, 2005.

31 Arana, 2001 and 2005. Also see www.seguridadpublicaenmexico. org.mx.

32 J. Londono and R. Guerrero, "Violencia en América Latina: epidemiología y costos" ("Latin American Violence: Epidemic and Costly"), IADB Working Paper, No. R-375, p. 22. Also see AID Paper, 2006.

33 AID Paper, 2006.

34 "U.S., Guatemala To Jointly Battle Crime," *The Miami Herald*, September 20, 2007. Also see Manuel Roig-Franzia, "Terms Set for Anti-Drug Aid from U.S., Mexico Says," at www. washingtonpost.com/w-p-syn/contest/article/2007/10/04.

35 *Ibid.*; Arana, 2005.

36 *Ibid.*

37 Bonilla, 2004.

38 AID Paper, 2006; Author Interviews.

39 *Ibid.*

40 *Ibid.*

41 Sullivan and Bunker, 2003, pp. 48-49.

42 *Ibid.*; Manwaring, 2005, pp. 9-10.

43 Arana, 2005, p. 101; Sullivan and Bunker, 2003, pp. 45-53.

44 *Ibid.*

45 Sullivan, "Maras Morphing," 2006, pp. 493-494.

46 *Ibid.*, p. 501.

47 Fishel and Grizzard, 2005, p. 4; AID Paper, 2006; Author Interviews.

48 *Ibid.*

49 In 2007, the United States gangs and drug trafficking in money is to help Central American governments draft a regional security policy. See www.cnn.com/2007/WORLD/Americas/07/19/ central.america.gangs .reut/index.html.

50 Reported by the Overseas Security Advisory Council, OSAC, December 12, 2005, at www.osac.gov/Maras/story.

51 Sullivan, "Maras Morphing," 2006.

52 AID Paper, 2006.

53 *Ibid.*; also see Mark Stevenson, "Mexico: Drug Gangs Using Terror Tactics," *Miami Herald*.com, May 17, 2007, at www. miamiherald.com/915/story/110509.html.

54 *Ibid.*; "Drug Gangs Set Their Sights on the Military," *El Universal*, May 15, 2007, at www.mexiconews.com.mex/Miami/ vi_24610.html; Kevin G. Hall, "Mexican Drug War Getting Bloodier," *Miami Herald*.com, March 21, 2007, at www.miamiherald.com/ 579/vprint/story/47875.html; "Mexican Gangs Terrorize Border," *CNN.com*, March 1, 2006, at www.cnn.com/2006/WORLD/Americas/ 03/01/mexico.gangs.reut/index.html; and David Jordan, 1999.

55 *Ibid.*; also see Sullivan, "Maras Morphing," 2006.

56 Sullivan, "Maras Morphing," 2006.

57 George W. Grayson, "Mexico and the Drug Cartels," Foreign Policy Research Institute, August 17, 2007, at www.fpri. org. Also see AID Paper, 2006.

58 *Ibid.*

59 *Ibid.*; also see "Mexican Drug Lords Use New Tools to Intimidate," *CNN.com*, April 13, 2007, at *cnn.worldnews.printthis. clickability.* ; and Duncan Kennedy, "Mounting Toll in *Mexico's Drug War,*" *BBC News*, July 5, 2007, at newsvote.bbc.co.uk/mpapps/pagetools/print/news. bbc.co.uk/2/hi/Americas/6250200.stm.

60 Manwaring, 2005, p. 24.

[61] Peter A. Lupsha, "The Role in the Invisible Wars," in Richard Ward and Harold Smith, eds., *International Terrorism: Operational Issues*, Chicago: University of Chicago Press, 1987; and Peter A. Lupsha, "Towards an Etiology of Drug Trafficking and Insurgent of Narco-Terrorism," *International Journal of Comparative and Applied Criminal Justice*, Fall 1989, pp. 70-74; and William J. Olson, "International Organized Crime: The Silent Threat to Sovereignty," *The Fletcher Forum*, Summer/Fall 1997, pp. 75-78.

[62] *Ibid.*

[63] *Ibid.*

[64] Jordan, 1999, p. 19.

[65] *Ibid.*; Arana, 2001 and 2005; Sullivan and Bunker, 2003; and Sullivan, "Maras Morphing," 2006.

[66] Jordan, 1999, pp. 142-157.

[67] *Ibid.*, pp. 193-194.

[68] "Five Slain in Nuevo Laredo, Pushing Year's Total over 100," *Houston Chronicle*, May 9, 2006, at www.chron.com/disp/story. mpl/world/3852351.html. This number was for the year in a city with a population of only 330,000.

[69] Stevenson, 2007; Hall, 2007; and Kennedy, 2007.

[70] Jordan, 1999, p. 152.

[71] Grayson, 2007. Also see Kristen Roberts, "U.S., Mexico Plan Billion Dollar Anti-Drug Effort," at www.News.yahoo.com/s/ nm/20071016.

[72] Ioan Grillo, "'Cop-killer' Guns from U.S. Seen Crossing into Mexico," *The Boston Globe*, August 19, 2007, at *www.boston. com/news/world/latinamerica/articles/2007/08/19/copo_killer_guns;* Duncan Kennedy, "Mounting Toll in Mexico's Drug War," *BBC News*, July 5, 2007, at www.newvote.bbc.co.uk/mpapps/pagetools/print/news/bbc.co.ul/2/hi/Americas/6250200.stm; "Armed Gang Kills Mexican Police," *BBC News*, May 17, 2007, at www/newsvote.bbc.co.ul/mpapps/gagetools/ print/news.bbc.co.uk/2/hi/Americas/6664215.

[73] Mary Beth Sheridan, "Traffickers Move into Yucatán Peninsula," *Los Angeles Times*, August 27, 1998. Also see Bunker and Sullivan, 2003.

[74] Robert J. Bunker and John P. Sullivan, "Cartel Evolution: Potentials and Consequences," *Transnational Organized Crime*, Summer 1998, pp. 55-74.

[75] Robert J. Bunker and Matt Begert, "Overview: Defending against the Enemies of the State, *Global Crime*, August-November, 2006, p. 309.

[76] *Ibid.*

[77] Sullivan and Bunker, 2003.

[78] Daniel C. Esty *et al.*, 1998; Robert H. Dorff, "Strategy, Grand Strategy, and the Search for Strategy," in Max G. Manwaring, Edwin G. Corr, and Robert H. Dorff, eds., *The Search for Security: A U.S. Grand Strategy for the 21st Century*, Westport, CT: Praeger, 2003, pp. 127-240.

[79] Olson, 1997.

[80] "Bubba, Bobo, Zambo and national Issues Fuel Gang Violence in the Caribbean," *The Economist*, November 4, 2004; Griffith, 1997. Also see John T. Fishel and Mary Grizzard, "Countering Ideological Support to Terrorism in the Circum-Caribbean," CSRC Discussion Paper 05/52, September 2005; William J. Olson, 1997; Fishel and Grizzard, 2005; John Rapley, "The New Middle Ages," *Foreign Affairs*, May/June 2006, pp. 93-103; and Author Interviews.

[81] These are terms used by former Brazilian president Fernando Henrique Cardoso, remembering *The Memoirs of a Militia Sergeant*, quoted in *El Estado de São Paulo*, September 22, 2006.

[82] "Gang Violence in the Caribbean," 2004; Griffith, 1997; Olson, 1997; and Rapley, 2006. An estimated 13,000 criminals have been deported from the United States since 1999.

[83] *Ibid.*

[84] *Ibid.*

[85] "Out of the Underworld," *The Economist*, January 27, 2006, p. 26.

[86] *Ibid.*; also see Fishel and Grizzard; and Griffith, and Rapley.

[87] Max G. Manwaring, *Gangs*, p. 10.

[88] "Anti-crime Community Initiative to Be Launched," *Jamaica Gleaner*, February 6, 2006.

[89] Rapley.

[90] *Ibid.*; and Author Interviews.

[91] *Ibid.*

[92] *Ibid.*

[93] "Beyond a Boundary," *The Economist*, February 24, 2007, p. 45; and Author Interviews.

[94] "Draft Declaration on Security in the Americas," approved by the Permanent Council of the Organization of American States at its regular session, held in Mexico City, Mexico, October 22, 2003, pp. 1, 3, 8.

[95] U.S.-CARCOM Update, "Secretary Rice Meets with Caribbean Officials to Discuss Democracy, Trade, and Security," March 24, 2006.

[96] Olson and Author Interviews.

[97] Jack Chang, "Gang Kicks Around Political Clout," *Miami Herald*, May 31, 2006; "The Mob Takes on the State," *The Economist*, May 20, 2006; and Julio A. Cirino, "Marcola, el jefe del area urbana fuera de control" (Marcola: The Boss of Out of Control Urban Areas"), *Investigación* , May 24, 2006.

[98] *Ibid.* Also see "São Paulo Violence Anniversary," *OSAC*, May 11, 2007, at www.osac.gov/Reports/reportcfm?contentID=68155& print.

[99] Abandoned by the state, *favelas* are city-states within the major cities of Brazil. They are feudal in nature and structure, and are noted as such in Rapley, "The New Middle Ages."

[100] A *jefe da favela* may be considered roughly equivalent to a feudal baron.

[101] Chang, *The Economist*; and Cirino, 2006.

[102] *Ibid.*

[103] *Ibid.*

[104] Cirino, 2006; *subir al cielo* also may be translated as "go up into heaven."

[105] Cirino, 2006.

[106] Police Colonel Elizeu Eclair, reported by *BBC News*, May 20, 2006, at news.bbc.co.uk/go/pr/fr/-/2/hi/americas/4999906.stan.

[107] Author Interviews.

[108] Peter Muello, "Militias Clean up Rio Slums," *The Miami Herald*, April 30, 2007, p. 8A.

[109] See Human Rights Watch statement at hrw.org/English/ docs/2007/06/29/brazil16298_txt.htm.

[110] "Fight in the *Favelas*," *The Economist*, August 4, 2007, p. 34.

[111] *Ibid.*; and author observation.

[112] Jennifer M. Taw and Bruce Hoffman, *The Urbanization of Insurgency: The Potential Challenge to U.S. Army Operations,* Santa Monica, CA: Rand Corp., 1994.

[113] Olson, 1997.

[114] *Ibid.*

[115] Sun Tzu, *The Art of War*, Samuel B. Griffith, trans., London: Oxford University Press [ca. 500 BC, 1782, 1910] 1971, pp. 77-78.

INDEX

D

E

F

G

H

I

N

O

P

Q

R

S

T